Against the Odds
Second Edition

Against the Odds
Second Edition

David-Lee Priest

Raceform

Dedicated to John Robert Parker Ravenscroft (aka John Peel)

DAVID-LEE PRIEST is a 28-year-old author and gambler living in Norwich and West London. He studied at Brunel University in West London, gaining a first-class honours degree in the Sport Sciences and a PhD in Psychology. In his spare time, David sings with a rock band and plays the guitar, piano, and saxophone. He competes in indoor athletics at the sprint distances of 60m and 200m. Aside from this he is an avid weight lifter, golfer, traveller, and reader who enjoys attending various sporting events around Europe. David is actively raising money for various charities by running the London marathon and undertaking a world record attempt that involves travelling the entire London Underground in the fastest possible time. Presently, he is writing a work of fiction.

Published in 2005 by Raceform Ltd
Compton, Newbury, Berkshire, RG20 6NL
Raceform Ltd is a wholly owned subsidiary of Trinity-Mirror plc

Copyright © David-Lee Priest 2005

The right of David-Lee Priest to be identified as the author of this work has been asserted by him in accordance with the Copyright, Designs and Patents Act 1988.

All rights reserved. No part of this publication may be reproduced, stored in a retrieval system, or transmitted in any form or by any means, electronic, mechanical, photocopying, recording, or otherwise, without the prior written permission of the publishers.

A catalogue record for this book is available from the British Library.

ISBN 1-905153-00-7

Cover design by Tracey Scarlett

Designed by Fiona Pike

Printed by Mackays of Chatham

CONTENTS

THE NEW EDITION

Welcome to the latest instalment of *Against the Odds*. If you're already familiar with the format then the major change that you will notice is a complete revision of the analyses. I haven't simply repeated the same tests; in many cases, I've refined the investigations that appeared in the first edition. The results certainly make for very interesting reading.

Although the introductory chapters are broadly similar in content to the original edition, there is plenty of new material. For example, I have added a new section on speed ratings and a comprehensive summary of my overall findings. *Against the Odds II* not only features information regarding the recent changes to the classification system of Flat racing, it also includes profit statistics for laying approaches.

In short, you will find that the 2005 edition is a bigger and leaner animal than its predecessor with keener eyes and a sharper set of teeth.

Have a profitable and enjoyable betting year.

David-Lee Priest
Stockholm
13 February 2005

FOREWORD

This in-depth analysis by David-Lee Priest is a must for anyone wanting to understand the complexities of betting and its surrounding language. Whether you are a seasoned punter or new to the betting jungle, you should study the theories and statistics in this book. The analyses in *Against the Odds* are both extraordinary and revealing; this book is yet another tool for punters in their ongoing battle with the bookmakers.

Michael Caulfield
Chief Executive of Jockey's Association (1988-2003)
and *Racing Post* columnist

INTRODUCTION

This book is about making a consistent profit from betting on the outcome of horse races. Somewhere in the recesses of every gambler's mind resides the pilgrim notion that betting can be made to pay. We all hear the call but not everybody answers. Some dismiss the thought before it has taken root. Some shrink away from the attempt in order to protect themselves from inglorious failure. Others commit themselves to making a profit; not all of those succeed, but none succeed who lack that conviction.

So why did you buy this book? Julian Wilson, the erstwhile anchor of the BBC's racing coverage, wrote that there are two approaches to betting on horseracing; the first is with a view to making money, the second is to regard it as entertainment. Like Mr Wilson, I follow the former approach. However, these two motives are not mutually exclusive. Winning money is fun, whereas the entertainment value of recreational betting is decimated when you leave all your cash with the bookmakers. Although the subject matter of this book may seem quite involved, spare a thought for those who study other fields of interest in the absence of any financial inducement to do so! Treasure maps would make geographers of us all.

WHAT'S IN A BOOK?
Salesmen would love us to believe that betting books are magic bullets that can be fired at the bookmakers. Indeed, this should be my cue to proclaim that *Against the Odds II* will save you its purchase price many times over. Yet curiously, books by professional gamblers who purport to reveal the secrets of successful betting are often advertised in mail-outs that are distributed to the clients of bookmakers. Surely, this is the equivalent of sending bomb-making kits to terrorists? Not so, because such books will suffer as many different interpretations as they have readers. That being the case, there must be thousands of different versions of *Against the Odds*; I hope that you're reading one of the better ones.

It was a book that galvanised my interest in betting and proved the catalyst that sparked subsequent success. It happened at very much the right time. I had just begun to attend racecourses again after a long absence and the dustsheets were being removed from those parts of my mind that dealt with betting strategy and equine performance. The crystal ball depicted on the cover spoke to me from the library shelf, foretelling of the improbable upturn in my betting fortunes. 'Forecasting Methods for Horseracing' followed me around the country. I read it at work, on the bus, in cafeterias, while sitting on park benches, on the London underground, at home, in railway stations, and in hotels. I didn't understand most of it. In fact, the book was peppered with esoteric mathematical formulae that I failed to grasp. Despite my lack of comprehension, or perhaps because of it, I was spurred on to mine the essence of what I was reading and exploit it for financial gain. What struck me most of all was that the author, Dr. Peter May, had developed intelligent strategies to solve the problem of predicting racehorse performance. Rather than simply feeding on the author's expendable store of ideas and methods, I decided to grow my own. It is not beyond the realms of possibility that someone who reads this book will receive the impetus to forge a career in betting. Maybe that person is you. In any case, you have just bought a ticket to the raffle.

THE READER

Probably the most important consideration for a writer is the reader of his work. The readership of racing and betting books is closely allied to the population of racegoers. Young people and women have traditionally been under-represented in such groups, but this balance is definitely changing. In keeping with the times, I have not assumed that all the participants in this book are male. Consequently, I have alternated the use of personal pronouns, i.e., his/her/his/her etc.

It is important that those who are new to horse racing and wish to develop their knowledge of betting are given the proper tools to do so. Poor betting performance is a prime reason that people may become discouraged and drift away from racing. Hence, I have written this book so that it is accessible to those who are new to the racing sphere. The racing tribe, as the anthropologist Kate Fox has christened us, possesses its own customs and language. For those freshly inducted tribe members who are still speaking this language with an accent, I have included a glossary to clarify the meaning of specialised terms and the identity of the various racing figures. Whatever your level of expertise, I hope to provide a valuable insight into betting and horse racing that will serve as a map to guide you across this most uncertain of terrains.

OVERVIEW OF THE BOOK

In writing this book, I chose a holistic approach to the issues that surround betting. I feel that the philosophy and psychology of betting cannot be segregated from the more earthly considerations that surround selection methods; they are all pieces in the same puzzle. For this reason, the book commences with a chapter that offers a fisheye view of gambling and its innate significance within our lives. Why do we gamble? I consider the reasons that underlie our desire to take risks. I feel it only fair to give you advanced warning that this section includes a sentence that begins, "millions of years ago our ancestors..." Don't worry, I haven't turned into Sir Robert Winston and I promise not to mention cavemen although I do refer to dingoes, tsunamis, quantum physics, sex, bullfighting, chaos theory, Nietzsche, and perhaps most mystifying of all, women.

The betting market is the essential context within which all backers must operate. Hence, a chapter is devoted to this subject. The sections that follow constitute the main body of the book; an appraisal of factors that determine the results of horse races. A computer database consisting of several years' racing results has allowed me to assess the impact of various criteria on racehorse performance and the profit that can be achieved from betting on certain types of runners under differing conditions. I have included many examples of profitable selections that may be used to form the basis of successful systems. However, I also take the opportunity to look beyond the statistics and present a more colourful and searching perspective on the themes in question.

The book continues with two chapters that focus on the practical concerns that relate to betting: selection systems, money management, the different types of bet that can be placed, and how to approach a day at the races. I conclude the chapter on betting with a full summary of the best techniques in the book as well as my essential profit guide. I end proceedings on an uplifting note as I consider the personal qualities that distinguish successful bettors from the crowd and explore the gratifying experience of backing horses successfully.

CHAPTER 1

The Philosophy of Gambling

"Gambling is a principle inherent in nature."

Edmund Burke, *House of Commons speech (1780)*

To truly understand betting we must place it on a broader canvas. If I don't stop to ask what gambling is and why I bet then I am like the scientist who develops the technology of cloning or destruction without pausing to consider the moral consequences of these actions. Everyone you have ever met or will ever meet is a gambler. Life involves the presumption of risk and thus we are gamblers all. The successful backer is a model of the successful human being; one who understands her immediate environment, effectively analyses risks and rewards, assigns realistic probabilities to events, makes good decisions based on her experience and judgement, and learns from mistakes.

RISK

It is human nature to seek out a certain degree of risk. In the sanitised world that we live in, this desire finds its expression in such phenomena as extreme sports and daredevil traditions like the Pamplona bull run, held in Spain every July. The desire to seek risk is a personal trait; not everyone would be suited to the life of a National

Pamplona Bull Run

Hunt jockey, for example. The experience of risk promotes a near instantaneous adrenal rush that can become addictive like an externally administered drug. Consider, for example, the behaviour of shoplifters, many of whom report that they steal not for the material value of their spoils but for what they perceive as the thrilling experience of evading apprehension.

ORIGINS OF RISK

"It can be argued that man's instinct to gamble is the only reason he is still not a monkey up in the trees" **Mario Puzo**

The explanation of risk-taking behaviour may lie with our ancestors. Millions of years ago, our forbears faced a constant succession of choices that determined their survival. It was mandatory to evaluate the threat posed by potential predators and an unknown terrain. In order to survive and mate it was necessary to make predictions and take certain controlled risks. Timidity and inaction would have meant a failure to acquire the resources needed to survive, whereas excessive bravado would increase the probability of a sudden demise. Hence, those who were successful at balancing risks with potential rewards were naturally selected, and it is from these individuals that we are all descended. The principle that I am referring to is demonstrated by the behaviour of the dingo during Australian bushfires. Fanned by strong winds, the fires sweep through the dry tinder and kindling of the forested outback. Almost the entire animal population, save for the very fast, are eventually consumed by the tall flames and perish. The awkward dingo does not possess the requisite speed to escape the advancing fires for very long. Whereas other species will flee from the flames, dingoes have been seen to stand their ground and charge directly through them. Upon reaching the other side, the beast will almost certainly end up with badly singed feet but he will survive thanks to taking a risk.

The link between this survival instinct and the behaviour of modern gamblers is striking. For example, the racecourse vernacular to describe the avoidance of losing one's betting capital is "staying alive". Indeed, the betting author Peter Braddock asserted that "betting can be seen as a hard, relentless struggle in which only the most able survive".

Humans in contemporary society express their gambling instincts through their financial decisions. The acquisition of financial resources underpins not only our survival but, to some extent, the quality of our lives. The decision to apply for a new job, purchase a house, or invest money reflects innate needs and drives that are vital to our prosperity and longevity. As with the case of our ancestors, competition for resources is high; not all can succeed, and many are haunted by financial worries throughout their adult lives.

RISK AND GENDER

The drive to find a mate and reproduce creates a context in which competition is high and it is necessary to gamble. Research has shown that females who are seeking a prospective mate place a very high value on a male's ability to acquire resources. Such resources increase the probability that the male will be able to provide for the female and their offspring. The flux of gender roles within society is altering the playing field to some extent. However, the instincts that drive females to select males, who can martial resources, stem from our ancestral lineage, and research suggests that these instincts still operate today. Consequently, it is incumbent upon males to take risks in order that they might acquire resources and thus satisfy the selection criteria of females. Conversely, females exercise selectivity and risk avoidance because their investment in the reproductive cycle (i.e., pregnancy and labour) is far greater than that of males (I'm too polite to say).

Notably, research into financial investments has revealed that women are more cautious than men regarding investment decisions and the purchase of financial products, while men are more apt to take risks. Although such attitudes are shifting, the patient and less impulsive attributes of women may actually dispose them to be more successful gamblers than men. As we shall see, **successful betting is about the careful management of risk**. Males vastly outnumber females in the ranks of bettors and gamblers. Legendary female gamblers such as Dorothy Paget provide the exception that neatly proves the rule. It is conceivable that the prevalence of men in the sphere of gambling may be partly explained by sex differences in terms of resource acquisition. However, gambling behaviour is also determined by socio-cultural factors. The ubiquitous gambling streak within racing culture has traditionally formed one of society's most patriarchal outposts. Accordingly, we might speculate that as gender roles in society change, the differences between the gambling behaviour of women and men will begin to dissolve as they have in the case of other behaviours such as consuming alcohol in public.

DECISION MAKING PROCESSES IN LIFE

At each moment, an infinite number of options and paths are open to us; life is a maze of astronomical proportions. Think of the impossible sequence of decisions that has constituted your own life. What has led you to the point of reading this book today? Allow me to use myself as an example: As a schoolboy, I remember electing to take GCSE physical education on the basis of a momentary whim, largely because my best friend had also chosen to take the subject. This subtle decision led me to study the sport sciences at university in London and subsequently encounter people who have changed my understanding of life completely. I am sure that you could cite a broadly similar chain of events from your own life.

Betting on horses draws on skills of risk management that have been honed in our everyday lives. Indeed, we must all take small risks at every moment and the seemingly innocuous decisions that are made on a minutely basis may have enormous repercussions. When you pack your bag for work in the morning, when you drive to a friend's house, when you buy food at the supermarket – you have options. It is in the nature of some people to consider these options very carefully and attempt to find the optimal way of performing every task so that there is some net gain or benefit. Others may drift through the day, routinely hitting bumps in the road of life and finding themselves inconvenienced and disadvantaged by events which they had failed to properly consider and prepare for. We are constantly honing the expertise to orchestrate the idiosyncratic patterns of our daily lives. In every decision we are assigning probabilities to events, evaluating risks, and balancing these risks with potential rewards. Due to the inherent uncertainty of life, we can only make the decision that seems most likely to be right at the time, based on our own assessment of the prevailing situation. There can be no knowing in a definite sense whether a decision was truly the right one, as there is a hidden price to every apparently fortuitous path. Tolkien expressed this idea somewhat more poetically when he wrote: "even the very wise cannot see all ends."

WINNING AND LOSING: SPORT AS A MODEL OF LIFE

Life and gambling are essentially about winning and losing. Both survival and reproduction require us to engage in competition with others and thus there are winners and losers at every turn. It is unsurprising then that we have evolved to derive much gratification from winning and much anguish from losing. Our lives are characterised by a succession of victories and defeats. We are drawn to the heat of competition. Indeed, it has been suggested that winning is the best feeling there is, and the second best is losing. Maybe there is some sort of innate gratification derived from the contest itself. Gambling is one of many ways that we symbolically recreate the drama of winning and losing. These instincts can be given free reign in the form of a relatively harmless pursuit. The sports that we bet on are, in themselves, models of competition, victory, and defeat. Philosophers have long suggested that in relatively peaceful times, sport offers a substitute for warlike competition. This being so, sporting teams now march into battle to the beat of patriotic drums, as once did soldiers.

Sporting teams function as people's elected representatives on the field of play. For example, a small-town football team that enjoys a fortuitous cup run seems to embody the hope and spirit of the community that it represents. The same phenomenon can be observed when a horse from a diminutive rural stable is fancied in a famous race such as the Grand National. The whole community links arms to support the steed that is running seemingly for them. Those who back horses are affiliated with their selected runner due to a financial imperative. However, just as in other sports, the horse is their appointed representative in the race.

Sport as warlike competition

Kate Fox explained that one of the delightful nuances of attending race meetings is the camaraderie that exists between those who have backed the same horse and share its fate. The affinity that backers, and indeed the general public, feel for certain horses can be boundless. Not so many years ago, I enjoyed a rather limited career as a college sprinter. Consequently, I feel an odd type of kinship with racehorses. I nurture the belief that, on some level, I know what they are going through. However, I was no great loss to collegiate athletics. My form record would have made very poor reading, possibly resembling the following: 004P20F. Nevertheless, I did have collateral form with Linford Christie. Maybe if human athletes were retired to stud like horses I would have been more incentivised. I have a theory that many racing enthusiasts would secretly like to be horses themselves. Before you dismiss this notion, envisage a well-developed and fully-fit sprinting colt. You are doubtless picturing a rippling statue of athleticism enveloped in swathes of muscle and positively shining with health and exuberance; the very paragon of power, youth, and virility; possessed of a beauty that fills the eye. Now envisage the inmates of a typical betting shop. I think I have made my point.

In an abstract sense, we can identify with horses because we are all running races of our own. Life is full of cruel obstacles and thus the public tends to reserve its greatest affection for jump horses. When a horse powers up the gruelling hill to victory at Cheltenham, battling bravely under twelve stones, I am reminded of people whom I have known. We are not so different to the horses. Will you stay on gamely under pressure? Will you fall at one of life's open ditches, and if so, how will you recover? Will you stick your neck out in a photo finish? Life is full of such questions to which we must all provide answers. This is especially true if you want to succeed in the sphere of betting.

CERTAINTY AND PREDICTION

"The subject of gambling is all encompassing. It combines man's natural play instinct with his desire to know about his fate and his future." **Franz Rosenthal, Gambling in Islam (1975)**

The will to predict is a characteristic of the human mind. Indeed, certain palaeontologists have proposed that the border between animal and human life was crossed when hominids first became aware of their own mortality and conceived of time in a sense that animals almost certainly do not. The burial practices of Neanderthal man some 70,000 years ago provided the first evidence that primitive humans possessed some knowledge of life and death. From this time forth, comprehending the inherent uncertainty of life has proved to be one of the banes of humanity; one that we have attempted to overcome through many means and doctrines, not least among them science and, arguably, religion.

The intended fruit of scientific exploration is knowledge of the physical world and, ultimately, the prediction of all phenomena. It is a great irony then that science has led us to a denial of certainty and prediction: The most famous idea of modern physics, Heisenberg's uncertainty principle, essentially states that, the more precisely the position of a quantum particle is known, the less precisely its momentum can be determined and vice versa. Hence, at the microscopic quantum level, the properties of particles cannot be measured exactly; rather, they are expressed as ranges of probability. Mercifully, the principles of quantum mechanics do not apply to the macroscopic world of everyday objects and events such as horseraces. In fact, it is more correct to say that the principles do apply but, due to the large size of directly observable objects when compared to sub-atomic particles, the range of uncertainty is so small as to be irrelevant. For example, the uncertainty in the position of a horse finishing a race would be something in the order of 10^{-31} mm, a distance so small that it is almost impossible to conceive of. What is interesting about Heisenberg's principle from a philosophical point of view is that, at the heart of nature, exists an inherent unpredictability that means our knowledge of reality must ultimately be limited.

Events at the macroscopic level such as weather systems and the orbits of stars should adhere to the principles of Newtonian mechanics and thus be predictable. Nevertheless, such phenomena are still partially subject to the uncertainty of the microscopic quantum world. An essential tenet of *chaos theory* is that minuscule changes in the starting point of a system (e.g., the weather) yield completely different outcomes. This knowledge gave rise to the theorem that a butterfly flapping its wings in Borneo could produce a hurricane in Florida. What if this chaotic tendency applies to horseraces? The implication would be that, if it were possible for the same race to be repeated many times over, very different outcomes may be observed. The number of variables that conspire to affect the result of a race defies comprehension and the race itself may unfold in an equally innumerable variety of ways.

Solving the conundrum that each contest provides is an activity that is enjoyed by millions because it appeals to our predictive and problem solving tendencies. As well as being a bane, the uncertainty of life is also a blessing because it creates so much of the excitement that characterises our experiences. This principle is wonderfully demonstrated by the thrilling climax of a race: an opportunity to anticipate and savour the living moment when uncertainty is resolved. Just as in life, there is little certainty in racing, a fact that is neatly expressed by the popular expression "racing certainty," meaning not quite certain.

The 19th century philosopher Friedrich Nietzsche wrote that science never really explains anything; instead, it merely provides ever more exacting descriptions. From a scientific viewpoint, there is never an explanation of why everything is the way it is, and this limitation is something that the foremost scientific brains of our times are entirely aware of.

Nietzsche

"The idea that this universe, in all its million-fold order and precision is the result of blind chance, is as credible as the idea that if a print shop blew up, all the type would fall down again in the finished and faultless form of the dictionary." **Albert Einstein**

Different Types of Betting Approach

CHAPTER 2

"Gambling: The sure way of getting nothing from something."

Wilson Mizner

Hitherto, I have used the words *bettor*, *gambler*, and *backer* almost interchangeably. In fact, most writers on this subject draw a distinction between the terms 'betting' and 'gambling'. Betting is regarded as the province of rational thinking; a considered investment, in which the bettor risks his capital when the probabilities of success can be estimated with reasonable accuracy. Conversely, gambling is a term that describes the indiscriminate and irrational wagering that is best exemplified by lotteries and casino games.

Those who write books such as this one invariably seek to associate themselves with betting and dissociate themselves from gambling. The concept of the 'mug punter' has become a ridiculous caricature in recent years and has come to represent the prototypical gambler, one "whose inept blunderings and disarray is the role most frequently associated with all who bet on horse-races" (Peter Braddock). When authors begin to heap contempt and derision on the mythical 'mug punter' in their attempt to differentiate themselves from his ilk, they sometimes stray towards a type of betting fascism that is unhelpful. It is more beneficial to realise that, as Alan Potts wrote, there is a mug punter in all of us. To exemplify this point I will invoke the distinction between the punter and the bettor that Peter Braddock drew in a 1983 book. It is important to clarify that the following descriptions are not caricatures that can be used to classify people into one category or another; rather, they are roles, which everybody fluctuates between to some extent. Hence, in reality these stereotypes do not exist.

BETTOR	PUNTER/GAMBLER
Decisive	Wavering
Responsive to circumstances	Unaware and slow to react
Flexible	Dogmatic
Emotionally detached	Emotionally involved
Unmoved by speculation and rumour	Driven by speculation and rumour
Aim of winning money	Addicted to the experience of gambling

BETTOR	PUNTER/GAMBLER
In control of betting decisions	Controlled by temptation of gambling
Takes responsibility for decisions	Blames others (e.g., the jockey or trainer)
Holds realistic expectations of success	Holds unrealistic expectations
Uninfluenced by recent good or bad fortune	Highly responsive to past results
Bets within means	Risks money she needs
Understands the nature of probability and uncertainty	Believes in luck and probability
Bets logically and rationally	Gambles illogically and irrationally
Trusts own opinions	Mistrusts own judgement
Sceptical of commonly held views	Follows fashion in a fickle manner
Self-aware	Deluded
Hard working	Lazy
Disciplined	Undisciplined
Committed to a course of action	Quits easily at the first sign of trouble
Accepts results with equanimity	Takes results personally

The significance here lies in the above descriptions underlying the terms 'betting' and 'gambling' rather than the actual terms themselves, which are used interchangeably by most people. The vast majority of those you meet will not care in the least whether you call yourself a gambler, a bettor, a backer, or a punter. There is no easy way out of the semantic jungle. 'Professional gambler' invokes a sinister and seedy image, whereas 'pro punter' just sounds juvenile and daft, something akin to being a 'pro tiddlywinker' for example. At least be thankful you're not in America, where the epithet of choice is "horse-player", a term that manages to be both ridiculous and disturbingly suggestive of bestiality.

Although the gap is shortening, research into equine performance and betting is far more advanced across the Atlantic than it is in the UK. Indeed, the growing influence of American literature on betting thought in Britain is exemplified by the use of American betting terminology in racing books written on these shores. Instead of betting according to a horse's draw we are now invited to "play the draw" as if it were craps or roulette. This is unsurprising given the current moves to conglomerate sports betting and casino gaming under the same umbrella.

A typology of successful betting approaches

Below, I have outlined three different types of successful bettor. The following categories are not intended to be discrete; they represent methodologies that every bettor may draw on to a certain extent.

The expert bettor

This expert bettor is a true racing enthusiast and student of the formbook. She keeps records of individual horses and develops an understanding of their various preferences and dispositions. Based on such knowledge, the expert forms clear opinions about the likely shape of a forthcoming race. She is a fine judge of a horse's appearance and manner and will incorporate such judgements into her betting decisions. By necessity, such knowledge is wrought from long experience and lessons learned. Consequently, the expert attends race meetings in person and will specialise in developing unique ideas and approaches that differ from those of the betting public in general.

The insider

The insider is an individual who is connected to a racing stable and is in a position to affect the training pattern and development of a horse. Hence, the insider is normally a trainer, owner, or somebody within the inner circle of a horse's connections. Such individuals typically operate in very small groups with the aim of preparing a horse to win a certain race in an organised fashion. To be successful, insiders must possess information regarding the horse's ability and fitness that is superior to that which is publicly available. Hence, a favourable price is obtained because a good performance is unexpected by bookmakers, journalists, and the wider betting public. This aim is often achieved by various machinations designed to cloak the true ability of an animal and reduce the public's estimation of the horse. For instance, there is no rule that prohibits a trainer from entering a horse in a race whose conditions are unlikely to suit the preferences of the animal in question.

True inside information is, by its definition, the province of very few individuals and is hardly ever the source of racecourse whispers or rumours, which can be dismissed as unfounded quackery. For example, telephone tipping services or racing newspapers would never be privy to such genuine intelligence. The vast majority of connections merely cajole you with optimistic blarney regarding the prospects of their charge. The trite observations that many inside gambles go awry and that two horses are often prepared for the same race are merely smoke screens akin to the old chestnut about crime not paying. I have never been involved with an inside gamble, but I have learned of several after the event, and such horses win very frequently at remunerative odds. An estimate from one stable suggested that a handful of such runners were sent out during the season, of which half would win at odds of over 5/1. It is quite possible to become an *insider*. However, the level of involvement and commitment required exceeds even that of the expert professional gambler. For those who are willing to push their way through closing doors, then this route represents the greatest possibility of long-term financial reward.

What approach do outsiders take towards inside gambles? One can either ignore them, as they are relatively seldom occurrences, or become familiar with the activities of smaller stables that depend on such gambles in order to survive financially. I take the former approach and accept inside activity as a negligible occupational hazard. Fortunately, I seldom bet in the types of races in which such gambles most frequently occur; namely low quality races (e.g., sellers), handicaps, and juvenile races that include many runners with unexposed form.

The systematic bettor

This type of bettor searches for patterns and trends among the data that are available in the racing media. The ultimate exponent of this approach might use a computerised selection system, which entirely removes the requirement for the systematic bettor to exercise his own judgement. Such an individual is more concerned with the relationships of abstract variables to profit than the real characteristics of a horse race.

J.P. McManus

All backers constitute a recipe of these three ingredients in varying degrees. For example, fabled professional gamblers such as J.P. McManus represent a mix of expert and inside approaches with the emphasis on the latter. My *modus operandi* is a blend of the expert and systematic approaches with an emphasis on the systematic, which is my real forte. Although there are few hard and fast rules, these different betting approaches are generally accompanied by different staking behaviour. Expert backers are limited in the number of bets they can strike because of the time involved in analysing form and their prerogative of searching for suitable betting opportunities. The insider will place very few bets during the course of the racing year, possibly as few as one. Hence, the stakes used are considered to be very large by most standards. The systematic backer is at the mercy of statistical trends, which she is betting will be repeated. Thus, in order to succeed, she generally needs to place a far higher number of bets with a correspondingly smaller stake so that statistical anomalies will not decimate her profit. This principle will be elaborated on further in Chapter 21.

The expert approach should be the keynote of every backer's technique. This admonition applies especially to the systematic backer, whose methodology can prove very ineffective if not galvanised by sufficient expertise. The methods of expert backers are often somewhat enigmatic and do not necessarily lend themselves to description or emulation. The instruction that is offered by such individuals functions as a pathfinder for the fledgling bettor, but the journey is long and arduous. It is basically incumbent upon the inexperienced backer to develop their own experience and judgement over the course of many years. The methods of an expert bettor are founded on long practice and a unique, counter-intuitive viewpoint; thus, they cannot simply be copied. Systematic methods provide an inexperienced bettor with some needed structure. However, there are pitfalls that accompany an over-reliance on the dogma of betting systems. In order to succeed, a complementary approach is required.

CHAPTER 3
Statistics

THE LIMITATIONS OF STATISTICS

The utility of statistics in racing is a subject that tends to divide experts. Some mistrust and debase statistics, some swear by them. However, if you take betting seriously, it is very hard to ignore them. An interesting parallel can be drawn with the use of statistics in psychology research. For the last few years, a debate has been simmering between those who advocate qualitative methods and the proponents of traditional quantitative research. Whereas quantitative data would consist of numerical responses such as those derived from a psychometric test, qualitative data might comprise interview transcripts or the observations of an expert. The crux of the debate is that these two schools of research represent entirely different world views. Quantitative research is based upon the doctrine that all phenomena can be reduced to simple cause and effect patterns that can be tested in a laboratory and thus quantified. However, those who advocate qualitative research paradigms typically recognise that reality is subjective and personal.

The researcher who follows quantitative methods would seek out underlying patterns that apply to all people. However, it has been argued that such patterns are meaningless abstractions from reality. After all, what does an average actually mean? Quantitative methods can become a parody of genuine science; consider for example the mathematicians who have devised a calculation to describe the state of romantic longing, an equation that always resolves into a negative number that indicates the degree of lack. Conversely, those who base their research on interviews and case studies normally work according to the principle that everyone is different and each individual can only be understood by comprehending what is normal for them. These two research philosophies touch on an essential paradox that applies to horses as well as humans: We are all the same and yet we are all different. How do you resolve these two opposing poles? The answer is surely that each method has its correct time and place; both are necessary to support a fuller understanding. Many betting experts treat each horse as a separate case and attempt to predict that horse's performance based on its idiosyncratic preferences. Other backers seek to compare all horses on the same numerical scale. Both of these approaches have their merits and you should consider which method is appropriate to the nature of the question that you are asking.

Statistics in themselves are devoid of meaning because they can be used to support contradictory arguments and theories. Like puppets, they can be made to dance as the statistician pleases. Hence, the interpretation that underlies a numerical pattern is very consequential. Despite their acknowledged limitations, statistics do provide a valuable tool to investigate patterns of racehorse performance. How many times have you heard assertive statements like the following: "two-year-olds who are well backed on their debut but finish out of the places are well worth supporting on their second run" or "sprint handicappers who re-appear quickly are always worth following." The data exist to test both these theories and that is the essence of this book. Why trust the same old received wisdom when you can test the veracity of such ideas yourself.

There is a clear analogy with science: One should form a hypothesis based on expertise and intuition. One should then design a method of testing this hypothesis using the data that are available. Finally, one is in the position to accept or reject the hypothesis and ultimately predict what may occur in future races. As with scientific exploration, it is just as important to know what doesn't work as it is to be aware of what does. Since the advent of internet-based betting exchanges, it is now possible to 'lay' a horse to lose as well as back it to win. Consequently, there is value in being able to ascertain when horses are likely to race poorly.

SAMPLE SIZE

A crucial dimension of statistical analysis is the sample size that is used. The majority of research into racing questions lacks a sufficient sample size to justify the conclusions that are drawn. Each year sees over 7,000 races held in the United Kingdom. Let us assume that we are looking for a pattern among the data that relate to these races. In the year 2004, 29.4% of favourites on the flat won their respective races. This percentage figure reflects the results of nearly five thousand races; thus, we might conclude that it is not the result of some freakish statistical aberration. However, if we divide that data into 50 small samples of 100 races, we find that the percentage of winning favourites varies from 23% to 52% across these smaller groups. Consequently, the profit or loss derived from backing favourites fluctuates wildly between groups.

Two or three individual results can dramatically alter the overall profit yielded in samples as small as 100 runners. It is not uncommon for an author to write: "to examine this theory, I tested it on the data from 107 races...." It follows that the most serious flaw attributable to many statistical analyses in the racing domain is an insufficient sample size. If we use a very large sample of races to examine a certain premise then the random distribution of results is evened out. For the same reason, we would be far more confident of achieving a 1 to 1 ratio of heads to tails after 10,000 tosses of a coin than we would after a mere 10 tosses. A conclusion based on a small sample is not necessarily invalid; it is just less likely to be an accurate reflection of events than a conclusion drawn from a much larger sample. In an ideal world we could harness a large sample to investigate every racing question that we cared to pose. In reality, we often have to accept a small sample size as a limitation.

A further factor worthy of consideration is time. Horseracing is a very fluid sport and its pattern of results is ever changing. This tendency is especially pertinent to the betting market, which is very responsive over time to organised betting activity. In simple terms, the market shifts to close any loophole that permits consistent profit (see Chapter 22). A large sample of data would typically include races that took place over a long period of time. Accordingly, it is not always possible to be confident that the results of such analyses would apply to future races because the conditions that led to the results and profits may have changed over time. An example of this phenomenon can be found in Chapter 18: I report the profits from backing horses that are drawn in specific starting stalls (e.g., stall 3 in 7f races at Kempton Park). Although I found many stalls that yielded a profit over a five-year period, remarkably few stalls produced a profit in each of the five years.

In fact, the draw is an extremely good example of the variability of results over time. The bias that exists at certain courses shifts due to turf husbandry and alterations in racecourse furniture (e.g., running rails, starting stalls). Furthermore, as a consistent bias becomes well known and backers begin to incorporate it into their betting strategy, the betting odds on offer alter to accommodate it. Where possible, it is important to include a time factor in your analyses. Quite simply, you are assessing whether the approach that you intend to follow has led to consistent profits, month on month, year on year. In conclusion, any statistical approach that is applied to racing represents a compromise and one must always be prepared to interpret the results with a critical eye.

An Investigation into Profitable Betting

THE 1978 ROYAL COMMISSION ON GAMBLING
In 1978 the government appointed a royal commission to investigate the issues surrounding gambling. The second volume of this report included an analysis of the potential for making profit from betting on the outcome of races. Information technology has progressed a long way since that time and far more searching analyses are now possible. However, the principle underlying the second volume of the report remains a very pertinent one. Such is the rationale for *Against the Odds*.

OVERVIEW OF THE FOLLOWING CHAPTERS
There are various factors that may be considered by a backer who wishes to bet on the outcome of a race. Some of these factors relate to the horse itself, such as age or fitness, whereas others concern the conditions of the race (e.g., the going or the draw). The following section of the book comprises a report focussing on several of these variables. The relationship that such variables have with equine performance and profit (or loss) will be presented in tabular form. An example of the presentation format is given in Table 1. The example is a notional one that serves to demonstrate the format.

TABLE 1. FINISHING POSITION IN PREVIOUS RACE				
FINISHING POSITION	N	SR%	P	VSP
1	3,560	24.6	£0.03	£0.12
2 – 4	10,420	14.1	-£0.12	£0.02
5 – 10	16,786	9.7	-£0.24	-£0.09
11 +	13,678	6.6	-£0.45	-£0.12
UNRACED	8,432	10.1	-£0.20	-£0.13

The tables are purposefully brief and contain only the most essential information. The title of the table includes the variable that is being related to performance and profit; in this case, the finishing position of the horse in its previous race. The 'N' at the head of the second column stands for 'number'. For example, 3,560 horses from this sample won their previous race (finishing position = 1). Of those runners, 24.6% won their following race; 'SR' stands for strike rate. To report the overall profit returned from staking a pound on each of those horses would be irrelevant. It depends how many horses were included in the sample: A profit of £100 produced by backing 12,000 runners would be negligible, whereas a profit of £100 generated by 50 £1 bets would be enormous by any measure. Hence, profit ('P') is given for every pound staked. This statistic provides us with a criterion to compare the profitability of different approaches. Thus, for every pound that was staked on horses that had won their previous race, you would have won 3p in the notional example. In the profit column, a minus figure indicates a loss. Hence, for every pound staked on horses that were previously unraced (bottom row of table) you would have lost 20p.

There are two reasons that the profit statistic is not completely reliable. Firstly, in a small sample, a winner at long odds (e.g., 20/1) will inflate the profit figure excessively. Secondly, when one is blindly staking a pound on each runner that fulfils a certain criterion (e.g., having won its last race) then money is wasted on longshots that have a meagre chance of winning their respective races. Other factors not accounted for by the narrow scope of the analysis affect the likelihood that a given horse will win its race, and these are reflected in the odds that are on offer. However, if one varies the stakes in such a way that the same amount would be won on each bet then this bias is eliminated. Hence, the stake would be £1 for a horse priced at evens, but 5p for a horse priced at 20/1 (£0.05 x 20 = £1).

The letters 'VSP' at the head of the final column stand for *Variable Stakes Profit*; a term that has been used extensively elsewhere to describe the type of staking that I have just explained. I will clarify in later chapters why it is a bad idea to adjust the level of your stake in this way when one is actually betting. However, as a diagnostic tool the VSP statistic helps to provide a more balanced assessment of profitability. In the text, I have often taken the liberty of reporting the overall profit returned when all selections of a certain type are backed with a £100 stake. I hope that this information will provide a more tangible description of the amount that might have been won in a series of real bets.

The analyses that I undertook whilst writing this book would have filled several huge volumes. Hence, in the interests of brevity I have taken the liberty of omitting tables and merely summarising results in the text where necessary. Similarly, there is insufficient space to discuss every last detail relating to the results in each table. There are occasions when you will need to cast your own interpretations of the results presented in the tables and accompanying graphs. Quite possibly, you will arrive at different conclusions to the ones that I have offered. In fact, I positively recommend that you do this.

For those who are interested in technical details, the samples that I have used consisted of flat races (turf and all-weather) between January 1999 and November 2004 and National Hunt races run from April 1999 until November 2004. Typically, I have used the entire dataset but in some cases I have only used a limited sample, e.g., only the 2004 season. In such cases, I have reported the specific sample that I used. The analyses of runners on the flat generally excludes all-weather racing, the results of which I have assessed separately.

THE DIFFERENT DOMAINS IN RACING

The races that comprise the annual fixture list are not a nebulous mass. Rather, racing is divided into discrete domains that can be thought of as functionally separate. The following statement is almost a consensus among the successful backers that I have encountered: Each category of racing is associated with different considerations and consequently requires a special approach. Hence, the analyses within the subsequent chapters are often undertaken separately for different types of races. In the following list, I will briefly introduce the distinctions that I used:

CODE: TURF (flat) / ALL-WEATHER (flat) / NATIONAL HUNT (jumps)

Flat racing and jump racing are quite rightly regarded as different sports. Likewise, all-weather flat racing is an entirely separate arena to its turf counterpart. The various artificial surfaces produce different patterns of results when compared to the turf. Generally, the ability that horses demonstrate on one surface does not transpose well to the other. When I refer to 'flat' races I will be writing about those run on turf. If I want to indicate all-weather races then I will do this explicitly.

Steeplechasing

All-weather racing

Hurdles

OBSTACLES IN NATIONAL HUNT RACES

Horses that run under National Hunt rules often begin their careers by competing in flat races that are known as 'bumpers'. This practice provides younger horses, which have not graduated from flat racing, with an opportunity to develop their racing skills and fitness levels prior to their first run over obstacles. Hence, bumpers are regarded as distinct from other National Hunt races and I have not included them in the majority of analyses that relate to jump racing as they distort the results of the tests. There is a marked qualitative difference between the two different types of obstacles that are used in jump racing; namely hurdles and fences. The fences that are used in steeplechasing present a far more rigorous jumping proposition than hurdles by virtue of their height but especially because of their relative rigidity. Thus, the technique used to jump fences is not merely an extension of that used to clear hurdles. As a consequence of these differences, I have analysed hurdle races and steeplechases separately in some instances.

HANDICAPS AND NON-HANDICAPS

The significance of this distinction should not be underestimated. The principle of handicapping horses with weight according to their perceived ability results in patterns of performance that are very distinct from those observed in non-handicap races. Indeed, handicaps are really a code within a code. It is more typical for a horse to run predominantly in either handicaps or non-handicaps than to oscillate between the two. Indeed, some horses become known as 'handicappers' due to their assimilation into this sphere of racing. All horses begin their careers in non-handicaps and subsequently progress through maiden or novice races against other less-seasoned opponents. If a horse shows consistent improvement and relatively high ability then it will continue to progress along the pattern of ever more competitive non-handicap races. However, most horses eventually find their way into the handicap fold sooner or later. Indeed, for the less able, handicaps provide the major opportunity for competition. The best handicaps of the year are extremely competitive and include some very able horses; this is especially so in National Hunt racing, where a high proportion of the fastest and most valuable races are handicaps.

AGE OF HORSES

In both flat and jump racing, horses begin their careers with a succession of races in which they compete against other juveniles. This framework enables younger horses to mature and race competitively before they acquire the requisite physical development to challenge their seniors. Juvenile races often yield distinct trends when analysed. In some instances I have considered it necessary to consider the performances of juveniles and older horses separately or focus purely on mature horses. In flat racing, a horse is eligible to race from the age of two. To simplify matters, all horses share an equine birthday on the first on January. Thus, no horse turns three during the flat season on the turf, which lasts from late March until early November. Two-year-olds seldom compete with their elders. Hence, it is a simple procedure to identify juvenile races. Flat horses continue to mature markedly during their third year also. However, for the purposes of analysis, I have identified two-year-olds as juveniles. In the case of jump racing, horses may begin competing in juvenile hurdles and bumpers at the tender age of three but it is equally possible that they join the National Hunt code from flat racing when older.

CONDITIONS OF RACES

Besides their status as either handicaps or non-handicaps, races are defined by various eligibility conditions that may alter their character. For example, the entrants may be maidens (yet to win a race), novices (inexperienced jumpers), or hunter-chasers (National Hunt horses that are licensed to participate in hunting). Some races are only open to horses of one sex. For example, the *Derby* is contested by colts and the equivalent *Oaks* by fillies. Races may be limited to amateur, apprentice, conditional, or lady riders. After 'selling' races, the winning horse is auctioned, whereas in the case of 'claiming' races, the weight borne by each runner is determined by the price that its owner is willing to sell the horse for after the race. Thus, the horses that are deemed to be the most valuable carry the greatest weight. There are other more arbitrary conditions that apply to a small number of races. However, the foregoing list encompasses all of the principal variations.

THE ABILITY OF HORSES CONTESTING RACES

Races are graded in terms of the ability of the horses that contest them. In National Hunt racing, Class A is the preserve of the elite and most able runners. From this peak, the scale descends towards the valleys of Classes G and H, which are the domains inhabited by the slowest and poorest animals. Class H comprises hunter chases and bumpers. Following a report by the British Horseracing Board's racing review committee, the structure of flat racing has been markedly changed from September 2004. The essential aim of the process was to simplify the classification system and align each division more closely to specific prize-money bands. Before the changes, there were wide discrepancies in prize money between races within the same division. In some cases, races were able to offer higher prize money than that which was available for contests that were supposedly in a higher grade. The previous division into eight classes (A-H) has been simplified into five grades. Class 1 is the equivalent of the former Class A, which includes the best races. At the bottom of the scale, Class 5 is the preserve of regional racing; a category introduced in January 2004 to provide opportunities for less able horses to compete. I have included a table to display the entire classification scheme.

TABLE 2. FULL FLAT CLASSIFICATION SCHEME. SEPTEMBER 1ST 2004				
Class	Race Types	3-y-o+		2-y-o
1	Pattern: Group 1	£200,000	*	£165,000
	Group 2	£100,000	*	£70,000
	Group 3	£50,000	*	£40,000
	Listed	£30,000	*	£25,000
	Heritage Handicaps	£50,000	*	N/A
	Conditions Stakes	£20,000+		£15,000+
	Handicaps 86-100 and 96-110			
	Classified Stakes 0-90 to 0-95			
	Novices			
	Maidens			
	Nursery Handicaps (£20,000+)			
2	Conditions Stakes	£10,000+		£8,000+
	Handicaps 71-85			
	Classified Stakes 0-75 to 0-85			
	Novices/Novice Auction/Novice Med Auction			
	Maidens/Maiden Auction/Med Auction Maiden			
	Nursery Handicaps			
3	Handicaps 56-70	£5,000+		£1,750+
	Classified Stakes 0-60 to 0-70			
	Novices/Novice Auction/Novice Med Auction			
	Maidens/Maiden Auction/Med Auction Maiden/Rating Related Maiden			
	Nursery Handicaps			
	Claimers and Sellers			
4	Handicaps 46-55	£3,500+		£1,750+
	Classified Stakes 0-50 and 0-55			
	Novices/Novice Auction/Novice Med Auction			
	Maidens/Maiden Auction/Med Auction Maiden/Rating Related Maiden			
	Nursery Handicaps			
	Claimers and Sellers			
5	Banded Stakes	£1,750+**		£1,750+**
	Maiden Auction/Med Auction Maiden			
	Sellers and Claimers			
*Minimum Total Prize Fund				
** A guide figure only; the total prize money of a six-race Regional Racing card must be £12,000				

In some instances, the races in these different strata of ability are governed by separate principles, and this is a factor that I have attempted to censor for at various junctures in the following chapters.

THE DISTANCE OF RACES

Many experts consider that different techniques are required depending on whether one is betting on the outcome of a sprint or a long-distance race. Indeed, it is not uncommon for a backer to posses a superior record when betting on races of a certain distance.

The Betting Market

BOOKMAKING AND THE CHARACTERISTICS OF THE MARKET

There is a point in most betting books when the author reveals, with some degree of self-congratulation, the "secrets of bookmaking" and proceeds to unveil a phalanx of charts and practical examples that leave you wishing you had never been born. Bearing in mind that such information is available from so many other sources I will present a simplified account of the betting market.

The principal on-course bookmakers trade from pitches either in the 'ring' that is situated in the Tattersalls enclosure or on the rails that segregate Tattersalls from the members' enclosure where betting is not permitted. The rails bookmakers are typically the most senior and established of their kind, and they form the epicentre of betting activity. Hence, the relatively small number of rails bookmakers exert a disproportionate effect on the market not least because they accept bets on credit from professional gamblers and other big-hitters. The see-sawing vibrancy of the betting ring is reminiscent of the heady bustle and passion of marketplaces in the developing world; an experience we've long since deserted for the sanitised delights of our chain stores and shopping malls.

The rails bookmakers

Bookmakers form a book by offering odds about each runner in a field. Bets are struck at the prices that are displayed on the bookmakers' boards. Hence, at the time of the transaction, both the backer and the bookmaker (layer) are aware of their potential profit or loss should the horse in question win or lose. There is a margin built into the bookmakers' prices, which is the mechanism that enables them to generate a profit in the long-term.

A betting ring

If one placed bets on every runner in a race so as to return £100 whichever horse won, the sum of the stakes would normally exceed £100; when this occurs, a book is said to be *over-round*. The over-round percentage is a statistic that describes the extent of the bookmakers' margin. If one needed to stake £110 to win a certain £100 by spreading one's stakes in the manner described above, then the percentage would be 110%. When this percentage is below 100, it is possible to make a certain profit by backing every runner in the book, in these rare cases the book is considered *over-broke*. The over-round book would ensure bookmakers a long-term profit if backers were to bet randomly. However, backers demonstrate a marked preference for the horses which are generally considered to have a greater chance of winning. Consequently, the bookmakers are in the position of constantly assessing their liabilities. These adjustments used to be a matter of deft skill but are now accomplished almost instantaneously by a computer software package that on-course bookmakers rely on.

To encourage backers to place bets on a horse, a bookmaker can adjust the price displayed on his board so that it compares favourably with those on offer by his competitors. Conversely, to effectively stem the flow of money that is being pledged in support of a fancied runner, the bookmaker need only reduce the odds about the horse in question to the extent that the price becomes uncompetitive. If a bookmaker's liabilities on a particular animal are great, i.e., an unacceptable loss would occur should the horse win, then he is in the position to lay-off the bets. Thus, any relatively large bets ripple through the ring, knocking over prices like dominoes. The on-course market is therefore properly regarded as a collective mechanism and it is difficult for any one bookmaker to differ markedly from the others without taking unacceptable risks.

The conservative approach of bookmakers resembles the herd mentality that is observed on the planes of Africa. Gazelles and Impalas know that their greatest chance of survival lies in forming a tight group and benefiting from each other's ears and eyes. An animal on its own is far more vulnerable to an attack by a cheetah or similar beast of prey. In bookmaking, the same patterns of behaviour exist; cautionary tales abound of naïve men who lost their entire capital on a single afternoon by drifting from the herd. Part of the reason for this conservatism is the existence of individuals who possess information that is unknown to the general public.

Only a very small percentage of backers (estimated to be between 1 and 2%) actually show a profit on a regular basis. Nevertheless, these sharper knives in the betting draw slice a sizeable portion off bookmakers' profits. Hence, it becomes imperative for bookmakers to balance the need to be competitive with the need to protect themselves from discriminate backers who will exploit any weakness in their prices. Essentially, the bookmaker is always attempting to minimise risk and render himself unsusceptible to individual results.

Due to the betting patterns of backers, the bookmaker is often in the position of facing a loss should the favourite win. Hence, his fortunes typically depend on how many favourites get beaten, and at what odds. The most astute and successful bookmakers adopt an enterprising approach of laying horses that they feel have a smaller chance of winning than the betting public presumes. By increasing their liabilities on such animals, they increase their profit margin should their opinion be proved correct. The majority of those who bet on the outcome of a race will do so off-course. Most of these bets are settled at the starting price (SP). The SP is determined by the board prices that are displayed by selected rails and betting ring bookmakers at the time of the off. Thus, in order to restrict their own liabilities, representatives of the large off-course bookmakers, such as Ladbrokes and William Hill, influence the market by placing bets on course. This practice reduces the SPs that are returned about runners which are heavily supported in the bookmakers' shops, through their telephone services, and on the internet.

The movement of the on-course betting market normally follows a predictable pattern. Initially, the prices about each runner are set to very conservative levels based on a 'tissue' that is compiled by industry experts. Some of these prices are incrementally lengthened (increased) in order to attract support for the runners in question. Finally, money that represents the interests of the biggest bookmakers is introduced a couple of minutes before the off in order to compress the prices once more. Hence, the market has an elastic property in that it expands and contracts. The smallest over-round percentages are to be found neither at the start of betting, nor at the off, but between 5 and 10 minutes prior to the race. Naturally, the pattern of support for each horse differs and that can be hard to anticipate.

To minimise the detrimental effect of price fluctuations on their profit, several backers I know divide their stakes and thus place several bets on the same horse. For example, you might bet half of your stake and continue to observe the movement of the market. Should the price about your selection remain unchanged then you would simply step in and place the remainder of your bet. However, should more favourable prices become available then you would be able to take advantage by placing further bets up to the value of your intended stake. Using this technique, you remove the pressure on yourself to obtain a favourable price in a single transaction and allow yourself several bites of the cherry. Hence, this strategy is one of risk negation and the more confident backers would risk waiting for the ideal moment at which to place their entire stake.

Let us examine the efficiency of the betting market by investigating the return that one can achieve by backing every runner that starts at a given price (see Table 3).

TABLE 3. STARTING PRICE (SP)						
	FLAT (inc AW)			National Hunt		
SP	N	SR%	PROFIT	N	SR%	PROFIT
Less than 1/2	685	72.6%	-£0.05	1028	75.2%	£0.75
1/2 – E	2308	54.9%	-£0.06	2722	55.2%	£0.55
E – 11/8	1942	44.6%	-£0.05	2107	44.0%	£0.44
6/4 – 2/1	5954	33.6%	-£0.06	6187	33.2%	£0.33
21/20 – 3/1	11470	25.0%	-£0.08	10564	24.9%	£0.25
10/3 – 4/1	11746	18.8%	-£0.11	9852	17.8%	£0.18
9/2 – 6/1	26561	14.2%	-£0.12	19880	14.4%	£0.14
13/2 – 9/1	20465	8.6%	-£0.20	13485	8.6%	£0.09
10/1 – 12/1	33902	6.4%	-£0.24	21698	6.5%	£0.07
14/1 – 16/1	34338	4.2%	-£0.34	20871	4.1%	£0.04
17/1 – 22/1	21010	3.2%	-£0.33	12828	2.8%	£0.03
23/1 – 33/1	38512	1.9%	-£0.45	24463	1.8%	£0.02
34/1 – 40/1	4812	1.0%	-£0.58	3546	1.1%	£0.01
41/1 – 1000/1	25718	0.5%	-£0.71	25487	0.5%	£0.01
All runners	255420	8.8%	-£0.30	186374	9.9%	£0.10

The 1978 royal commission undertook a similar examination and found that returns became increasingly poorer as the odds about the runners lengthened. Indeed, over a long period of time, backing horses that started at 4/6 or shorter actually led to a profit. Conversely, the less-fancied runners produced an abysmal rate of return if backed blindly. This type of analysis has been undertaken in the last two decades by many academic researchers. The results are always very similar and the prevailing trend is now referred to as the "favourite-longshot bias".

Many reasons have been advanced to explain why longer-priced horses offer a much lower return than favourites. I favour the following explanation: Bookmakers must achieve their over-round percentage in some way. If the return derived from backing market leaders was very poor then the lack of value would appear obvious to backers. It is less noticeable to offer unfair odds about the runners that few backers will be supporting as opposed to the favoured horses that are driving the market. Furthermore, bookmakers are forced to compete to a greater extent in order to attract money for

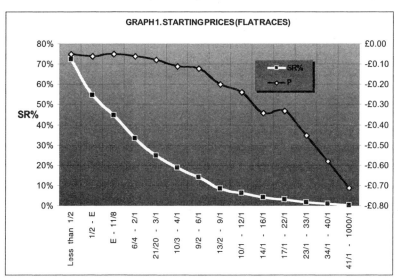

runners at the favoured end of the market where the lion's share of money is staked.

In Table 3 we can see that SPs are highly accurate predictors of performance. The shorter the price about a horse, the greater the chance it will win its respective race. However, after reviewing many similar analyses, it is clear that the favourite-longshot bias is softening somewhat, especially in recent years. Longshots have always generated a hideously poor return. However, the bias is levelling out at the favoured end of the market. This trend is particularly evident when we examine Graph 1. Only when the prices rise above 6/1 do the returns really begin to decrease. Until this point, the increase in loss is quite gradual. For example, if you had backed every horse priced at 1/2 or lower on the flat then you would have lost

5p (per pound staked) whereas the loss is still only 12p for runners priced between 9/2 and 6/1. Although Table 3 provides a useful insight into the dynamics of the market, it is important not to interpret the findings too literally and simply back odds-on shots because they show the best levels of return. These results would only apply to those who are backing horses blindly, which is the antithesis of the approach that I advocate.

PRICES AND BETTING STRATEGY

"I put my money on the longshots … I went from lukewarm to hot" **Jay-Zee, rapper**

What we can surmise is that we have a mountain to climb if we want to back horses at long odds. The vast majority of these runners have a snowball's chance in hell of winning their races. The longshots that do oblige are often the beneficiaries of some fortuitous accident or other factor that defies anticipation. Nevertheless, the most astute professional backers do include longshots in their betting strategy and many of them would advise you to do so as well. The reason for this is that, despite the obvious risk of losing your entire capital, backing longshots creates an opportunity to generate large profits that simply does not exist when supporting runners offered at more modest odds.

When you consider yourself to be fully fledged, your ability to return a profit from your longer-priced selections will be the mark of your proficiency. However, until that glorious day I recommend that you adopt a more conservative approach. Even if you do become adept at backing longer-priced selections, you must realise that the opportunities will be very few and your strike rate will still be relatively low (around 10%). Hence, longshots should always be the icing on your betting cake.

Let's cross the street and consider horses that carry the shorter prices. Don't back them under any circumstances. This may seem like strange advice when viewed in the light of the information in Table 3. However, a very similar principle is at work: Just as it is hard to convert the exceedingly poor returns yielded by longshots into profit, the increase in strike rate that is required to make a reasonable profit from backing favourites is immense in real terms. Alan Potts explained this very well in *Against the Crowd* and confirmed the belief that I have held since I was a boy, so I can do no better than relay his reasoning.

Approximately 44 out of every 100 even-money shots win their respective races. Hence, in order to break even you must find another six winners. Furthermore, in order to make a healthy profit (let us say 20p per pound staked) you need to find another 10 winners. This means that you need to produce a 60% strike rate when the horses that you are looking to back typically win only 44% of their races. What prevents you from doing this? The inherent uncertainty of horse races. In simple terms, every horse is susceptible to what Dr. Peter May referred to as 'the accident factor', regardless of its price. A worrying host of ailments and misfortunes can afflict any horse without warning. For example, in chases, 8.5% of odds-on favourites fall, unseat their riders, or refuse to jump. Have you ever endured that sinking feeling after a backing a short-priced favourite that appears to be carrying a fridge on its back? You know the one I mean: He starts poorly, gets steadily worse during the middle section of the race, and the less said about the end the better. "The gelding was never travelling," reports the jockey. Well that's alright then, I don't mind losing my thousand quid now I know that the gelding "wasn't travelling" – that explains everything.

In the final analysis horses are animals not machines, even those runners that are confidently expected to win. This simple truth contributes almost as much to bookmakers' profits as the over-round book. Banks and other financial institutions must know about the accident factor too, as they gleefully secrete inflated charges within the small print of their agreements. The week your mother goes into hospital and you are a few days late paying your credit card bill, they've got you to the tune of £25, money you might have worked hours to earn. The principle that underlies these mercenary charges is the same one that favours the bookmakers: Life is full of uncertainty and every now and again even the most organised people and horses slip up – it's a statistical probability.

The inherent uncertainty that governs races renders the very notion of betting at odds-on intuitively ridiculous. Indeed, I am sure that there are tribesmen from the recesses of the amazon valley, as yet untouched by civilisation, who would counsel you not to bet at odds-on. However, the old dogma does not stretch far enough. Avoiding odds-on horses and betting at 11/8 or 5/4 is like locking your front door but leaving your windows wide open. It is remarkable that, the more successful a bettor is, the more likely he is to refuse to bet at prices under 3/1.

If you shouldn't bet at short prices and you shouldn't bet at long prices then which runners can you back? There are good reasons to avoid longshots and even better reasons to avoid skimpy prices, so it follows that there is a middle ground where prices are more likely to offer the potential of profit to the backer. After years of analysis and examining the results of my own bets with great scrutiny, I have set my personal limit at between 4/1 and 8/1. The reason for this is that my profit levels have been consistently healthy within this range but they drop dramatically either side of it; probably for the reasons that I have outlined above.

I find it almost eerie when I contemplate how many successful backers have independently arrived at exactly the same conclusion that I have. Your personal limit may differ to mine depending on your own betting performance and your level of comfort with risk. For instance, you may choose to back horses at odds of between 5/2 and 13/2 or 5/1 and 12/1 with some longshots if you dare. In any event, ensure that your range is not too restrictive. The spread of prices that I favour includes about 23% of all runners; even this is pushing it a little bit. A certain amount of caution is required. If you have a sensational record backing horses starting at 9/2 but struggle with 4/1 or 5/1 chances and you are thinking of favouring horses priced at 9/2 then think again. Prices in the region of 9/2 are quite volatile in the betting market and what you have uncovered is a statistical anomaly.

SP PERCENTAGES

I investigated SP percentages (the over-round percentage of the official starting prices) in order to ascertain how they were affected by different factors. The principal influence on SP percentages is the number of runners in a race; small fields produce much lower SP percentages. Envisage a two-horse race. If the SP percentage were too high then both runners would be heavily odds-on and appear to offer appalling value. As the number of runners increases, the fairness of the prices becomes harder to discern. Furthermore, a large field is likely to include several longshots; the animals about which bookmakers offer the least fair prices. Even though I accounted for the number of runners in each race, I found no difference in SP percentages between the different codes of racing, handicaps and non-handicaps, and valuable races and minor races. Table 4 demonstrates the expected relationship between SP percentages and field sizes. There are minor aberrations. For example, bookmakers increase the SP% for races that the public tends to gamble on (e.g., the Grand National). For similar reasons, the SP% on bank holidays, when crowds are large, tends to be less than generous.

TABLE 4. SP PERCENTAGES (Flat)		
RUNNERS	N	SP%
1-3	166	106.5
4-5	1,496	111.8
6-7	2,869	115
8-10	5,253	119.9
11-14	5,848	126.9
15-20	4,009	137
21 +	579	147
All runners	20,220	124.7

I decided to assess the extent to which the SP percentage of a given race affected the returns produced by backing horses in different price brackets. The results are presented in Table 5. Because of the high correlation between the SP% and the number of runners in a race, this table should also provide an indication of the returns derived when betting in fields of different sizes. Depending on the prevailing SP%, odds-on favourites return a loss of between 0p and 32p (per £ staked); this represents quite a discrepancy. Within the sample, 390 odds-on favourites ran in races where the SP% was higher than 126. The returns from backing these runners was so poor that if one had simply opposed them on a betting exchange by 'laying' (more about this later in the chapter) then a very comfortable profit of around 14p (per pound staked) would have followed.

TABLE 5. RETURNS ACCORDING TO SP% OF National Hunt RACES					
	SP %				
SP	under 112%	112 - 118%	118 - 126%	126 -140%	over 140%
Under Evens	-£0.04	£0.00	-£0.03	-£0.12	-£0.32
E – 2/1	-£0.04	-£0.09	-£0.07	-£0.11	-£0.16
9/4 – 4/1	-£0.09	-£0.12	-£0.14	-£0.18	-£0.20
9/2 – 6/1	-£0.07	-£0.08	-£0.11	-£0.16	-£0.09
13/2 – 17/2	-£0.07	-£0.17	-£0.20	-£0.19	-£0.28
9/1 – 10/1	-£0.10	-£0.22	-£0.19	-£0.22	-£0.44
11/1 – 14/1	-£0.15	-£0.12	-£0.26	-£0.28	-£0.42
15/1 – 20/1	-£0.29	-£0.32	-£0.31	-£0.44	-£0.55
22/1 – 500/1	-£0.49	-£0.53	-£0.61	-£0.62	-£0.76

If we glance further down the table then we can see that runners in the 9/1 – 10/1 bracket return a loss of between 10p and 44p depending on the SP% of the race; a very big differential. In summary, it is advantageous to bet in races where there is a low SP% regardless of the market's opinion of the horse that you wish to back. If all other factors are equal then the lower the SP%, the more favourable the price about your selection. Betting in races with low SP percentages typically means betting when there are relatively small fields. It is often said that such races yield unpredictable results, as they are not run at a true pace and can often be overtly tactical in nature. However, there is little indication of this anticipated unpredictability save for the fact that odds-on horses actually produce better returns when running in races with a moderate SP% as opposed to a low SP%. In both flat and National Hunt racing, odds-on horses are not as profitable to follow in races with small fields (e.g., < 6) as they are in races with medium-sized fields (e.g., 6-12 runners).

WIN BETTING WITH THE TOTE

When you place a win bet with the tote, your stake is added to a pool. After the race, this pool is divided between those who select the winning horse. Bettors receive dividends in proportion to their original stake. Whereas the SP percentage fluctuates, the tote always deducts 13.5% from the win pool prior to payout in order to cover its costs and statutory contribution to racing. This deduction would equate to a 115.61% SP percentage. Hence, when the SP percentage is likely to exceed 116, there is a greater likelihood that a given tote dividend will improve upon the equivalent starting price. Clearly, the dividend is not determined until betting closes. Consequently, your return on a winning bet can be drastically lower than the price which appears on the screen at the point when the bet is placed.

The size of tote win pools is such that even modest bets of £30 can drastically reduce the dividend in some cases. This tendency deters the more serious backers. Highly popular races such as those run at the Cheltenham festival generate large pools and provide the exception to this rule. In fairness to the tote, the win pools have increased in the last year, principally because of a decrease in the deduction made. The fall from 16% (= SP% of 119.05%) to 13.5% means that the tote win bet currently beats the SP in the majority of cases whereas the opposite was formerly true.

Betting with the Tote

A particular section of the gambling public favours the tote over the traditional bookmakers. Their number includes those who will invariably back the favourite, a heavily tipped horse, the charge of a well-known trainer, or the mount of a popular jockey. Consequently, the dividend on these obvious selections is invariably lower than the equivalent SP. It follows that the relative profitability of betting with the tote depends on the type of selections that you typically make. A simple rule of thumb is to pay especial attention to the tote win dividend if the horse you aim to back is either priced higher than 6/1 or running in a large field; such races tend to have a higher SP% whereas the tote deduction is always the same. The Grand National is a good race in which to consider the tote win bet as traditional bookmakers offer an SP% that is often as high as 145. Hence, the tote bet beats the starting price in most years. For example, Bindaree returned an SP of 20/1 in 2002 yet the tote win dividend equated to 33/1.

At the end of 2004, I reviewed all the bets I made during the year and ascertained that I was right not to bet with the tote. Nevertheless, you can never truly rely on such an analysis because your own stake money would have altered the dividends. Certainly, my triple figure stakes would have triggered meltdown at some of the smaller tracks at which I bet.

THE BETTING EXCHANGES

Without question, the most meaningful event in the recent annals of betting history is the emergence of the exchanges. For once, all the hyperbole and rhetoric is justified because the betting market has been fundamentally and irrevocably altered. We know this by watching the larger bookmakers. They have sailed through every other technological innovation and supposed threat to their interests with smug indifference. However, with the advent of the exchanges, the layers began to throw their toys out of the pram.

Betting exchanges, such as Betfair, Betdaq and IbetX, provide a brokerage allowing bettors with opposing viewpoints to match each other's bets. Each backer is paired with a 'layer' who effectively accepts the backer's bet in the role traditionally played by a bookmaker. The exchange acts as a mediator and thereby precludes the layer from taking part in unlicensed bookmaking. If the layer is successful then he retains the backer's stake; whereas, if he is unsuccessful, he forfeits the backer's winnings. Much like transactions with an on-course bookmaker, both the backer and layer know their liabilities at the time a bet is matched.

Betting online with an exchange

The option of laying creates a whole new theatre of operations for the bettor. As you will already know, it is far easier to find losers than winners! Indeed, the former outnumber the latter by a ratio of almost eleven to one. An essential component of successful betting is the ability to confidently eliminate horses from consideration, especially those runners that are favoured and thus occupy a large percentage of the market. In fact, the skills that underlie backing and laying are a perfect compliment to each other.

Because the longer-priced runners in a race would normally yield the lowest returns, it might seem prudent to lay them. There are several reasons why this is not advisable: Firstly, the exchange markets are much fairer than those formed by conventional bookmakers and this fairness is most evident in the prices of the less-fancied runners. For example, it is quite normal to find an exchange price of 20/1 or higher about a runner whose SP is 14/1. There is a margin between the backing and laying prices that are available on the exchanges. This is equivalent to the 'spread' that occurs in stock market trading and in spread betting. Hence, one cannot simultaneously back and lay a runner for the same price.

The margin depends on the price of the selection. For example, if the horse that you wish to back is priced at evens, you will often be able to lay it at a price only fractionally above that, e.g., 21/20. However, the market becomes dramatically weaker as your eyes descend the screen toward the less able. A margin of four points or more about a longshot is not uncommon. This means that you may only be able to lay our 14/1 SP runner at 25/1 or worse! You may decide that this is still a good betting opportunity because, in your opinion, the race could be re-run until the end of time without the sorry beast obliging. However, I would still caution you against the wager because you are effectively betting at 1/25! Otherwise expressed, you are risking a loss of £25 to win £1. If just one of these lays goes awry then you will spend the rest of the season repairing the damage. It just does not make any financial sense.

A further compelling reason to concentrate on laying the more fancied runners is that you will be able to bet with respectably large sums. To lay outsiders on a betting exchange will often enable you to win just a few pounds. Hence, the exchanges suffer the same blight as the tote: It is not easy to bet large sums in small races. I prefer to lay horses with shorter prices (generally below 2/1). If you follow my example then your liabilities will be manageable and even if you are betting at odds-on, you can sometimes have as many as 25 horses on your side; therefore the 'accident factor' seems to work in your favour.

Exchanges provide you with a great deal of flexibility when placing your bet. For example, let us assume that you wish to back a horse that is an 8/1 chance with the bookmakers. On an exchange, you may be able to stake up to £300 at the same price and £76 at the more favourable price of 17/2. If your intended stake is £100 then you could place the first £76 of this amount and leave the remaining £24 as an 'order' at 17/2. Once you have left your cheese out in the wind like this, you can watch from a safe distance to see if anyone who wants to lay your selection matches your bet. Depending on how optimistic you have been when setting the price of your order, you may be first in the cue to be matched or somewhere towards the rear. While your bet is unmatched you can cancel the order, alter the stake, or adjust the price that you are willing to accept.

Placing bets with an exchange has the feel of stock market trading and after some practice one can become very adept at reading the flow of the market. The volatility of the market generally works in favour of the shrewd backer. This is especially true of the range of prices that I would accept about a runner (i.e., 4/1 – 8/1). I have sometimes managed to beat the SP by as many as four points, taking 12/1 about an 8/1 chance. This differential is so large that your profits can be massively increased. Indeed, using the exchanges in this way enabled me to show a profit during a month when my selections yielded a loss at the SP. The real fillip for me is the fact that I can place speculative orders at 4/1 (the lowest price that is acceptable to me) when the bookmakers are trading at around 3/1 on a given runner. This is the equivalent of having a *conditional* bet; an option that most bookmakers would deny you with impunity.

If my order remains unmatched then it matters not because I would never bet at 3/1 in any case. If I do get on then I have obtained a fantastic price by default. On one occasion I was even able to get 4/1 about a filly that never went above 3s in the ring and started at 5/2. To steal one and a half points at the business end of a very weak market is the sort of manoeuvre that one would like to have stuffed and displayed in a cabinet for all to see. Indeed, if I were able to obtain a price of 4/1 on every runner that started at 5/2 then I would reap a glorious 45p profit on every pound I staked. The flip side to this coin is that I sometimes inexplicably fail to get on. I can recall an occasion when I left an order for my usual stake at 4/1. Owing to the fact that the odds about my selection touched 4s in the betting ring, I assumed I was safely on. I am sure you can guess what happened next. My bet was never matched and the horse romped home. This failure to have my bet matched probably owed much to the size of my stake and a particularly weak market. The moral of the story is that unmatched exchange bets are like children in supermarkets – not to be left unattended. If you feel the need to conduct a little research into the movement of the market then utilise the facility that some of the exchanges allow you whereby it is possible to view the fluctuation of a given price over time and observe its peaks and troughs.

A further advantage of the exchanges is the flexibility of betting when it pleases you. For example, if I want to bet on a race at a small meeting on a Wednesday afternoon that I cannot attend then I would ordinarily be tied to the phones or the internet waiting slavishly for the market to open. To make matters worse, although the on-course market opens some 15 to 20 minutes prior to the start of a race, it is not uncommon to wait until five minutes before the off to obtain a price over the telephone. In addition, a little research has shown me that the prices relayed from the track rarely seem to reflect the best odds that could be obtained in the ring itself. If I were betting through an exchange, I could comfortably review all the markets during the morning and place my bets accordingly should I care to do something else in the afternoon. The flexibility that the exchanges provide is especially valuable to those who are otherwise occupied during the day, i.e., most of the betting public. Before the emergence of the exchanges it was incumbent on you to bet on-course if you wanted the best prices; this is no longer the case.

The exchanges have created large ripples in the overall betting market. I am often given to positioning myself behind a busy bookmaker's pitch in the ring and observing the goings on. I can cast my eye over his laptop screen to discover where his liabilities lie and which horses the punters are choosing to support. During these educational sorties, I am intrigued to note how the bookmakers are constantly comparing their prices to those available on the betting exchanges and exploiting any discrepancy. This mechanism effectively links the on-course and exchange markets under a single umbrella. A defining characteristic of all betting markets is their plasticity: Any discrepancy between prices creates an obvious opportunity for profit; hence prices are apt to cluster. Consequently, I have found that there is rarely a great advantage in backing horses on the exchanges immediately prior to a race. I have enjoyed greater success by monitoring the prices earlier during the day of the race.

When you bet with a conventional bookmaker you are competing against other backers. As many observers have pointed out, the successful bettors win the money that other backers have lost. So it follows that to be successful, a far greater number of others must be unsuccessful. In the case of the betting exchanges, this principle is even more acute. There is something pleasing about going head to head with a fellow bettor who holds the opposite opinion to your own.

One drawback that attends exchanges is the commission you must pay on winning bets which varies from between 2 to 5% depending on various loyalty schemes. The simple rule is that you must factor the commission into the price when you bet: a throwback to the dark ages of betting tax! Firstly, the exchanges deal in decimal prices which include the nominal £1 stake; i.e., evens = 2.00, 5/2 = 3.5 etc. If you can achieve 4/1 (5.00) about your selection with a bookmaker then you need to obtain a price that is between 2 to 5% higher in order to account for the commission. Thus, at a price of 4/1 (5.00), commission at the level of 5% would increase the price by .2 (4 x .05) from 5.0 to 5.2. Such a calculation is very simple to perform and when you bet frequently on the exchanges you will know these increments by heart in the same way that a darts player knows his outshots. Table 6 (opposite) contains a small list of equivalent prices to demonstrate the principle:

TABLE 6. CONVERSION BETWEEN FRACTIONAL ODDS AND EXCHANGE ODDS PLUS COMMISSION			
FRACTIONAL ODDS	EXCHANGE ODDS + 3%	EXCHANGE ODDS + 4%	EXCHANGE ODDS + 5%
EVENS	2.03	2.04	2.05
2/1	3.06	3.08	3.10
4/1	5.12	5.16	5.20
6/1	7.18	7.24	7.30
8/1	9.24	9.32	9.40
10/1	11.30	11.40	11.50
12/1	13.36	13.48	13.60
14/1	15.42	15.56	15.70
16/1	17.48	17.64	17.80
20/1	21.60	21.80	22.00

Whereas 'betting' shops appear to have been configured to promote gambling tendencies, the exchanges seem to have been designed to meet the needs of the betting public. Consequently, it has become easier in the few last years for the discerning bettor to make a profit. Unfortunately, the data I use for my research does not include betting exchange prices or market moves; all the following tables and profit figures are based on SP returns. When betting on-course, the SP can nearly always be beaten. Hence, the profit figures I have produced for various approaches are somewhat conservative and you should take this into account as you appraise them. If a certain type of approach yields a profit of 5p (per £ staked) then opportunities would exist to increase this level of profit by several pence, especially in the case of selections that start at relatively long odds.

Despite the lack of data relating to exchange prices, I formulated a method that enabled me to provide profit / loss figures for laying. As I explained, I prefer the conventional approach of laying short-priced horses as this reduces the liability one faces. At odds below 3/1, the margin separating the laying and backing prices is generally quite small; if a horse can be backed at a decimal price of 2.00 (evens) then, providing the market is relatively strong, it might be laid at odds of between 2.02-2.05. Based on this assumption, I have conservatively estimated that the laying odds in each case are 5% greater than the starting price. For instance, if the starting price is evens then my estimate of the laying price would be 21/20 (2.05). In reporting my results, I will refer to a certain level of *profit per pound staked*, i.e., the amount that would be lost if the selection were to win the race. For example, if I laid a horse that was trading at 1.5 (1/2 as fractional odds) to lose £100 then I would profit £200 if the animal failed to win. Accordingly, my profit would be 200p per pound staked.

Handicap Ratings CHAPTER 6

The official system of handicap ratings is based on the concept that all horses can be assessed on a numerical scale that enables them to be compared according to their ability. The scale ranges from 0-140 on the flat and 0-175 over the jumps. The higher a horse is rated on the scale, the more able it is considered to be by the handicapper.

The exact position a horse occupies on the scale is determined by its performances against other animals; the number of (horse) lengths it is beaten by and the distance by which it beats others. Thus, the unit of the scale would be lengths other than for the fact that horses race over vastly differing distances (e.g., 5f to 2m6f on the flat). Whereas a single length advantage would constitute a very narrow victory in the Grand National (4m4f), it would be considered far more decisive in a 5f sprint. Because of this, the unit of the scale is lbs, which relates to the saddle weight that horses bear. The simple premise is that weight slows horses down; a proposition that I will discuss in detail in Chapter 8. It is thought that, as race distance increases, so does the effect of a given weight. For example, according to the scale, a single pound of weight equates to around one third of a length in a 5f sprint but just over one length in the case of a race contested over two miles. I estimated these figures by using a simple equation (below) that affords us an approximate value. However, the techniques that real handicappers use are somewhat more sophisticated.

$$\text{Lbs beaten} \quad = \quad \frac{\text{Distance beaten in lengths} * 15}{\text{Distance of race in furlongs}}$$

At regular intervals, the handicapper will review the performance of each horse and adjust the animal's rating depending on how it fared in relation to the other horses it raced against. Such calculations take into account the effects of weight. For example, if horse A beats horse B by 5 lengths over 7.5f (equates to 10lb) but horse B carries 10lb more in saddle weight than horse A, then the performances are considered equal.

The subtleties of handicapping comprise an art rather than a science and the subjective opinion of the handicapper often comes into play. For instance, handicappers often use race times to assist them in the evaluation of unexposed horses on their first few public outings. On other occasions, the handicapper would focus on a reliable or consistent horse and use this runner as a reference point against which to compare the performances of improving animals. The grade of a race and the quality of performance normally associated with this grade may also be taken into account when assessing form. Thus, handicapping presents a minefield of dialectic alternatives and constitutes a model of selection in itself. In America, the term *handicapping* has a more generic use and refers to the entire process of assessing form and predicting racehorse performance.

There are different types of handicap ratings: The official mark is compiled by the BHB (British Horseracing Board) and is used as the basis for allotting weight in handicap races. Several other private handicaps exist, some of which are affiliated to newspapers such as 'postmark', the rating produced by the *Racing Post*. The remits of the private and official handicappers are quite different. The aim of the BHB handicapper is to engender competitive racing and consequently the ideal potential of a horse is assessed. Private handicappers are not accountable to the interests of the horse's connections and therefore have a lot more latitude in determining their mark. Because of this, private ratings normally reflect what a horse has actually achieved rather than what it is potentially capable of.

I undertook a series of analyses in order to assess the relationship of Raceform's performance rating to profit. In order to assess the relationship between ratings and subsequent performance, I used a technique advocated by Peter May. I determined the top-rated runner in each race based on the mark achieved by each horse in its previous run. I then gave a score to every runner in the race based on how many lbs below the top-rated animal it fell on the scale. Thus, to the top-rated runner I gave the score '0' and to a runner that was rated 10 lbs lower, I gave the score '10', and so on. In handicap races, additional saddle weight is used to impede the more able horses. Hence, I used non-handicap races to form the sample. Graph 2 displays the results of the ratings analysis for National Hunt races.

The results are a testament to the utility of the rating system and the skill of the handicapper. Indeed, the Raceform ratings that I used marginally outperform the betting market in terms of predicting profit and performance (strike rate). The top-rated runners and those rated within 3lb of them almost returned a profit. This is quite an impressive result when one considers that there are over 12,000 such runners in the sample. If we follow the white line indicating SR% then we observe a sharp dip between the marker points that represent the top-rated runner and those rated 1-3 lbs adrift. Whereas a top-rated horse may be many lbs clear of its closest rival, a horse that is rated within the 1-3 lb bracket always has a top-rated animal to compete against. Although winning a lot less frequently, horses rated 1-3 lb adrift of the top-rated horse return a similar profit. This may be because top-rated runners are overbet by the betting public thereby reducing the odds. The data relating to flat races paints a different picture in that, while top-rated runners produce a profit of 2p (per £ staked), runners rated 1-3 lb adrift return a loss of 14p.

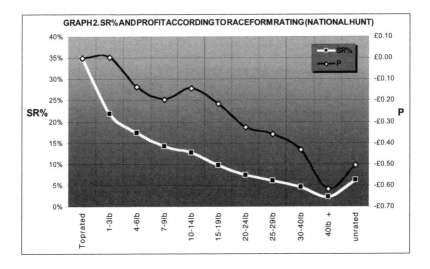

GRAPH 2. SR% AND PROFIT ACCORDING TO RACEFORM RATING (NATIONAL HUNT)

Runners that are rated 40 lbs or more behind the top-rated runner have an abysmal record. Indeed, the poor performance of lowly-rated horses can be used as the basis of a profitable laying approach. If one had laid the 496 runners rated 10lb or more adrift of the top-rated horse and starting at 2/1 or less then a profit of 16p (per £ staked) would have ensued. If one had laid each of these selections to lose £100 (should the horse in question have won) then a total profit of £7,936 would have been banked over the five-year period of the sample. Where I live, that's nearly enough to pay for the water bills.

The returns produced by top-rated two-year-old horses were outstanding: 1,300 of the 3,715 such runners in my sample won (SR of 35%) yielding a profit of 7p per pound staked. If each of these selections had carried a £100 stake then a profit of £26,005 would have followed. When considering a bet in two-year-old races you may want to pay slightly closer attention to horses that are rated within six lbs of the highest-rated animal as these selections also produced a profit. For those interested in specifics, I did operate some rules in making the above selections: For example, I didn't include ratings from a previous season. Nor did I include races where less than four runners were rated. Also, if the highest-rated selection in a race had achieved a mark of less than 60 then I excluded that race from the analysis.

The ratings I used were the ones derived from each horse's most recent performance. I also took the liberty of testing different statistics based on the horse's best performance (from its last six races in the current season) and the average of its last three performances (within the current season). One would expect that each of these methods would yield a more powerful predictor of performance than a statistic based purely on a single run. However, the SR% of top-rated horses was noticeably higher in the case of the ratings derived from the most recent run. Nevertheless, the difference in profit obtained by using the three methods was negligible. All of the above goes to show the value of recent form (i.e., the horse's previous outing), even if this form appears to be accounted for by the prices that the bookmakers offer.

LIMITATIONS OF HANDICAP RATING

Despite the obvious utility of handicap ratings, they are fraught with limitations and in order to present a balanced view I have reported these below.

1) The 'Aintree' factor. In 2002 there was something of a furore when Ginger McCain's *Amberleigh House* was excluded from participating in the Grand National because his handicap rating was too low. Owing to the fact that the range of weights that the runners are permitted to carry is limited, horses with relatively low ratings in relation to the most able horse in the race are effectively excluded from competing. If this constraint were strictly adhered to then the Grand National would have a field of only 16 or 17 runners. Thus, the handicapper allocates weights for the famous race with a view to including as many runners as possible. The controversy was caused because the animal in question had produced an excellent round of jumping over the unique Grand National fences in winning the Beecher chase at Aintree some five months previously. Hence, due to the special jumping requirements of the great race, the trainer felt that the ratings should have been re-interpreted to account for *Amberleigh House*'s jumping ability. The above example was retained from the first edition of *Against the Odds* (2003) with good reason: *Amberleigh House* went on to win the National in 2004, totally justifying Ginger McCain's prior faith in his horse. Indeed, research at Liverpool University has verified the Aintree factor: Horses with experience of jumping the Grand National fences have a greater chance of success when compared to those enjoying their virgin outing over the formidable obstacles. The only silver lining to the above saga was that McCain was interviewed by an unsuspecting Clare Balding on daytime television in the aftermath of the disputed decision and used some olympic-standard 'colourful' language in making his opinions felt.

2) The effect of the draw skews ratings. This factor is completely ignored in the compilation of most handicaps. Hence, a horse may possess an artificially low rating because he has been hampered by a succession of poor draws.

3) The distances that separate horses that finish down the field are exaggerated because only the principals in a race are likely to expend full effort towards the finish. Once his chance has gone, a jockey will often spare a horse instead of driving it out. Money for the minor places in lower grades of competition is not exactly breathtaking. Hence, the above comments may apply to horses finishing as

Amberleigh House

Ginger McCain

high as second in a race with poor prize money. Conversely, form in the more prestigious races is somewhat more reliable owing to the fact that genuine competition ensues for the minor placings.

4) Un-rated horses present a problem for the handicapper. The ratings produced for very inexperienced and lightly-raced horses are notoriously unreliable. Furthermore, horses with foreign form such as the stream of juvenile hurdlers that cross the channel from France, are very difficult to evaluate. One solution to these issues is to bet in races where débutants and foreign horses seldom appear, such as higher quality conditions races on the flat for three-year-olds and upwards.

5) The pace of the race affects the veracity of the result. True races that are competitive and run in a fast time will produce results that accurately reflect the difference in ability between horses. Conversely, races that are tactical, slow, and non-competitive will yield outcomes that fail to demonstrate the true merit of the runners. For example, in a slowly-run race that yields a blistering sprint finish, the field may pass the post in a cluster that unduly flatters some of the weaker horses.

6) Some handicappers do not take into account the subjective components of a horse's performance such as the ease with which victory is gained. Similarly, a handicapper may ignore problems that a horse encountered in running which robbed the animal of vital lengths.

7) The methods used to compile ratings evolve over time. Hence, the marks that are produced in 2005 may not be commensurate with those dating from 1995. It is especially important to remember that, while ratings are based on analytical methods, they do also reflect the subjective opinion of the handicapper and are thus liable to a further source of variation. For example, the *Racing Post*'s private handicap has performed better since 2002, when Simon Turner began to share the responsibility for postmark selections with established handicapper Paul Curtis.

8) The going (state of the ground) can radically affect the distances that separate horses at the conclusion of a race. When the ground is heavy (very muddy), winning distances can be highly exaggerated. On all-weather surfaces, the pattern of performance is somewhat different and fields generally finish with greater distances separating them.

By far the most serious weakness that can be attributed to performance ratings is the way in which weight is incorporated into the calculations. This is the subject of Chapter 8.

CHAPTER 7
Speed Ratings

An alternative to scales of ability that are based purely on margins of victory and defeat are speed ratings, which are determined by the times that horses take to complete their races. The advantage of speed ratings is that they constitute an absolute measure against an objective standard.

As with private handicap ratings, speed figures are of particular importance in certain types of races. Races on turf are often resolved by a sprint finish and are not always 'truly run'; hence, slow times do not always indicate a lack of ability. Conversely, all-weather surfaces do not permit the same level of acceleration that turf does and consequently races are run in a more evenly-paced manner. It follows that speed figures are of prime importance when considering a bet in an all-weather race.

COMPILATION OF SPEED RATINGS

There are many methods of concocting speed ratings but they share common foundations. Rather than relay an abstract formula or specialised approach I offer a very simple account of the mechanics that underlie speed figures in general. Without question, a time recorded in a 5f race on the sweeping downhill track at Epsom is not comparable with a time clocked on the stern, uphill 5f course at neighbouring Sandown. Due to the different characteristics of each racecourse, it is necessary to correct race-times in order to take into account for the *standard time* that applies to each distance that is run at every racecourse. There are different ways of compiling a standard time. For example, the term often refers to the time that would be expected of a moderate horse (e.g., rated 100 on the flat) when carrying ten stones in weight and running on good ground.

For each race we arrive at a speed figure that expresses the winner's performance in relation to the standard time (number of seconds faster or slower). The speed figure must be expressed *per furlong* in order that races of varying distance may be compared. For instance, a performance over a mile that is one second under the standard time would equate to a time two seconds below standard in a two-mile race and so on.

Understandably, race-times are slower when the going is soft. Indeed, 'slow' and 'fast' are considered to be categories of going in some racing nations. The influence of the ground on times is accounted for by calculating a *going allowance*: The times for each race on a given card are compared to standard times in order to assess the extent to which today's clockings are collectively slower or faster than expected. Standard times are not the only reference point that can be used when determining the going allowance. Instead, it is possible to compare today's race-times against those recorded in similar races at the course in question (e.g., maiden races for three-year-olds in Class 3). Once calculated, the going allowance is used to correct the speed figure by effectively eliminating the influence of the ground.

For the sake of clarity, the final speed figure is normally converted into the same scale of weight that is used in conventional handicap ratings. This procedure results in a rating for the winner of the race. To determine the ratings for each other runner, points are deducted according to the distance (in lbs) that the horse was beaten by the winner. Because the weight scale is used, the differences in saddle weight between the runners can then be accounted for in manner described in the previous chapter.

SPEED RATINGS VS. HANDICAP RATINGS

In general, I find that speed figures do not bear as good a relationship with performance and profit as handicap ratings. Thus, I do not make extensive use of race-times in my betting approach. However, I stress that this is my personal choice and it is one that many successful backers would not concur with. Indeed, most experts exhibit a preference for either speed ratings or traditional handicap marks. For this reason, opinions on the subject have become rather polarised.

My antipathy to speed figures probably stems from the fact that they are more complex to compile and assess than handicap ratings. Consequently, there is more that can go wrong. In particular, I find the establishment of standard times a somewhat inexact science that is open to many inaccuracies, especially when published race distances are often incorrect due to the movement of running rails etc. Furthermore, the going allowance for each fixture has to be calculated from a very small sample size and is thus subject to the vagaries of individual races, not all of which may be truly run. A further conceptual criticism is that the standard times and going allowances must be defined in relation to each other creating a circular formula. In other words, in order to ascertain the standard time one must eliminate the influence of going; whereas, in order to assess the going allowance, one must incorporate standard times or some equivalent. In short, I find speed ratings to be a method with too many moving parts. Alternatively, it may simply be that I am very poor at compiling them.

A PROFITABLE BETTING METHOD BASED ON RACE-TIMES

Despite my reservations, I readily concede that the concept of assessing performance according to the objective criterion of race-times is appealing. There is no doubt that, when expertly compiled, speed ratings provide adept backers with a decisive edge. I think the reason for this is that the conventional handicap scale is somewhat exposed; it is quite easy for most punters to discern the distances that have separated horses in previous races, even if it is necessary to use collateral form. Hence, handicap ratings are generally incorporated into the prices on offer and opportunities for profit are limited. Race-times on the other hand are relatively hidden from view; it is unusual for them to be discussed at length in the racing press. When speed is referred to prominently then this is normally because of a fast time (e.g., a course record) that could simply have been due to firm ground. The standard time and going allowance that may affect a race-time are rarely brought into the discussion. Furthermore, it is not immediately apparent from watching a race whether a fast time has been recorded or not.

To exploit this blind spot in the betting public's field of vision I have cobbled together a simple method of basing selections on race-times. Like all profitable approaches, the aim is not simply to identify horses that will perform well but to obtain favourable odds by identifying selections that are overlooked by the betting public at large. It is somewhat ironic then that the method I have developed depends solely on information that could be gleaned in a few minutes from the *Racing Post*! This is exceptional and the general rule is that to produce a profit using widely available information is extremely difficult.

Essentially, I sought to circumvent the twin problems of standard times and going allowances by waiting until I found a race with two runners which had recorded recent times that could be directly compared (i.e., same course, distance, and going). This is not as rare an occurrence as intuition dictates it should be. Quite often two horses will visit the same course and run in similar contests in preparation for a big race. It is debatable whether one can say with confidence that two horses have indeed raced over similar ground (see Chapter 14 for a further discussion). However, this limitation is the only real fart under the duvet; as long as the two races in question were run at the same course then minor discrepancies between the two distances and going reports can be tolerated. For example, if two hurdles races, the first over 2 miles and the second over 2m 1f, were both held at the same course on good ground, then there would be some basis for a comparison of the times. Of course, it is not enough simply to find an occasion when two runners in a certain race have recorded recent times under similar conditions: The real rub is to pinpoint an unexposed or unfancied horse that has produced a time that is similar to or better than that recorded by one of the market leaders in a race.

THE SPECTROSCOPE AFFAIR

Around the time that the first edition of *Against the Odds* was published, I used the above method to pinpoint one my biggest ever bets. I will always associate the

Cheltenham Festival of 2003 with the Jonjo O' Neill gelding *Spectroscope*. The Triumph Hurdle is one of the most competitive races in the sport's calendar. Run over 2m 1f, it takes the form of a cavalry charge contested by a large field of unexposed, rapidly improving juvenile hurdlers, many of whom would have recently migrated from flat racing. I had seen the second favourite *Well Chief* four weeks earlier at Kempton running in a preparation race that normally provides good indications for the Triumph Hurdle. On that day I had been very unimpressed with the German-bred, Martin Pipe gelding. He won a meandering two-mile lope of a race that it would have been nearly impossible for him to lose. I remember thinking that I could not envisage an event less like the Triumph. Indeed, one race reader wrote that the contest bore about as much resemblance to the Cheltenham race as Coronation Street does to Macbeth.

Martin Pipe's runners remain in their winter coat (unclipped) longer than most and his juveniles rarely please the eye, but even so, Well Chief really stood out in the paddock for all the wrong reasons. He looked frail and awkward. On the day of the Triumph, the bare form must have looked respectable on paper and the betting public latched on to the gelding, backing him down to 7/1. I resolved to oppose Well Chief days before the race, but with what? I had been toying with the notion of supporting the bay gelding Spectroscope who had recorded a victory in a stronger-run contest at Kempton over the same trip, some 15 days before Well Chief had graced the Surrey course. What really interested me was the difference in the available odds. Although boasting a similar form record to the heavily fancied Well Chief, Spectroscope was hovering around the 25/1 mark. This strange differential had much to do with the twin reputations of trainer Martin Pipe and his heroic stable jockey at that time: Tony McCoy. The form relating to the Triumph Hurdle is labyrinthine to say the least. Consequently, during the period leading up to the race I was still juggling several alternatives to Well Chief, who looked as unsightly as ever in the paddock. I had reached something of an 'indecision frontier' and was on the verge of reluctantly bailing out of the race when I decided to check the recent race-times of the leading contenders. The black print stopped me in my tracks. What I saw is reproduced in Table 7.

TABLE 7. SPECTROSCOPE vs WELL CHIEF				
RUNNER	PREVIOUS RACE	GOING	RACE-TIMES	PRICE FOR TRIUMPH HURDLE
SPECTROSCOPE	FEB 7. KEMPTON 2m NOV. HURDLE. CLASS A(2)	GOOD TO SOFT	4m 2.55s	7/1
WELL CHIEF	FEB 21. KEMPTON 2m NOV. HURDLE. CLASS D	GOOD	4m 6.2s	25/1

Spectroscope

What really caught my eye was the fact that Spectroscope had recorded a faster time than Well Chief on slower ground. I literally sprinted to the ring (all the training finally came in useful) and found a smiling face ready to offer me 33/1 about the Jonjo O'Neill gelding. There was only just time to take up a position on the members' lawn. Spectroscope swept through the field and held off a fierce challenge from Well Chief under Tony McCoy to win by a head, although it might as well have been a country mile. What makes this example so relevant is not that I predicted that Spectroscope would run as well as his rival, but that nobody else did. I was able to obtain 33/1 about a horse whose starting price should have been in single figures. In this instance, a simple analysis of speed had afforded me a real edge on the betting public.

My lasting memory of that day was not of the race itself but of the crowd. Quite understandably I punched the air with my fist and circled round, only to be met by a silent sea of gritted teeth. They'd all backed the McCoy horse and were about as happy as a bunch of bastards on fathers' day. That may seem like a rather vain thing to mention but it strikes at the heart of the point that I'm making. You can't afford to have sympathy for the losses of the general public, because without their losing, you can't win. Aside from the famous trainer and jockey, I think that what led the crowd to follow Well Chief that day was the fact that he had won a Class A (grade II) race at Kempton as opposed to Spectroscope's Class D. Hence, the supposed class of the two races had belied the real merit of the performances. In my opinion, this exemplifies the best way to utilise speed ratings: to identify a horse that has won a seemingly poor race in a fast time. The betting public would simply not expect that a gelding which had won a Class D juvenile hurdles race could beat a rival who had taken an equivalent race at a much higher grade. I have laboured this example long enough, but for good reason; it perfectly demonstrates the very essence of what I aim to do as a gambler.

I had good call to remember Spectroscope at Aintree the following year. The Grand National meeting in early April serves as an excellent restorative to combat the post-Cheltenham blues. I always look forward to this particular stop on the racing merry-go-round. Liverpool is a vibrant and characterful city to stay in, the racing is of a very high quality, and the craic is mighty as my Irish friends say. If you're contemplating a visit then make sure you've got a grandstand seat for the Saturday and preferably the Friday as well, otherwise you won't be able to move. Also, be warned that ladies day can be quite a hormonal experience; I've had to ban myself from betting due to the sheer weight of distractions. Horses for once are beaten into second place, albeit in a photo finish.

Ladies day at Aintree

The Liverpool Long Distance Hurdle is Aintree's equivalent of the Stayers' Hurdle (aka World Hurdle) that now heads the Thursday of the Cheltenham festival. In 2004, the heavily odds-on favourite for the Aintree race was Iris's Gift, recently crowned at Cheltenham. The year before, I had backed the grey at 7/1 to usurp Francois

Doumen's mighty French gelding Baracouda in the Stayers'. He went down by three quarters of a length but in 2004 the placings were reversed and I got my revenge. Although I'd followed Iris's Gift for two years, I thought nothing of deserting him at Aintree: There should be no place for sentimentality to muddle your judgement in betting. I had good reasons to back up this decision: Cheltenham festival form transfers very poorly to Aintree. There is simply not enough rest for most horses between the fixtures and the two courses are utterly different. The price of 4/7 about Iris's Gift left me with little doubt that I should oppose Jonjo O'Neill's charge.

Royal Rosa

There appeared to be two main challengers: the smart six-year-old *Sh Boom* who had been fancied in the Stayers' at Cheltenham until falling and the unexposed French gelding *Royal Rosa*. The pair had met at Haydock on January 10th, on which occasion Sh Boom had emerged the victor by eight lengths. Perhaps for this reason, Sh Boom was priced at 5/1 making him the stark second favourite and you could bet Royal Rosa at 11s. What intrigued me was that Royal Rosa had returned to Haydock on February 28th and won a race almost identical to that in which he had faced Sh Boom 50 days earlier. The first race had been only Royal Rosa's second dash over hurdles. Hence, I reasoned that the French horse was improving and, remembering Spectroscope, thumbed through the Racing Post to look at the race-times. Table 8 tells the tale of the tape:

TABLE 8. ROYAL ROSA vs SH BOOM				
RUNNER	PREVIOUS RACE	GOING	RACE-TIMES	PRICE FOR LIVERPOOL HURDLE
SH BOOM	JAN 10. HAYDOCK. 2m7.5f. NOV. HURDLE.	GOOD	6m 4.0s	5/1
ROYAL ROSA	FEB 28. HAYDOCK. 2m7.5f. NOV. HURDLE.	GOOD	5m 46.4s	11/1

I thought Sh Boom quite uppity in the Cheltenham race so I was more than happy to support Royal Rosa at a healthy price of 12/1. In this respect I was proved completely right. Unfortunately for me, I was wrong about my old friend Iris's Gift, the 4/7 chance produced what racing pundits described as the 'performance of the meeting' to close out Royal Rosa by two lengths. "Poetry in motion," were the words of one hack. Imagine my wild applause. Despite the fact that I had lost this bet, it represented a very solid wager at the time it was struck. If it were possible to pick 12/1 chances that were able to challenge right up to the line in every race then long-term profits would surely follow. The only bitter taste in my mouth was that, bearing in mind the obvious supremacy of Iris's Gift (if he were to have recovered fully from Cheltenham), I could have easily bet on Royal Rosa to beat the rest of the field (i.e., without the favourite) at the healthy price of 4/1. I even had the option of taking out an insurance policy by betting each-way. Based on what I knew about the speed of the Haydock races, I really should have made some sort of profit from the Liverpool Long Distance Hurdle that year.

The Effects of Weight

Is it valid to express the differences between horses in terms of lbs? The manner in which weight is factored into handicap ratings would seem to suggest that the effect of weight on performance is a universal constant.

Consider the case of two horses of precisely equal ability. Now assume that these hypothetical charges could run an endless succession of 5f races without fatigue. If the first horse were to carry an extra pound of weight, would it really lose the hypothetical race by the exact one third of a length that the handicapper predicts it should. Furthermore, if one kept adding weight to the saddlecloth of the first horse, would the animal proceed to lose each race by a margin that was in exact proportion to weight added? Would this principle operate similarly for all horses of different physiques in a universal way?

A fully-trained thoroughbred

A fully-trained racehorse can weigh well over 500 kg (78.5 stones). In the trained thoroughbred, as much as 50 per cent of the bodyweight is constituted of muscle; the equivalent of a human bodybuilder. The horse's quadrupedal gait, strength, and efficiency of movement make it marvellously suited to bearing loads; a characteristic that has defined the human-equine relationship for thousands of years. What difference is a three pound penalty really going to make to animal of some 1,200 lbs, especially when the animal in question is a beast of burden and the weight is well positioned above the horse's centre of gravity? The eminent backer Nick Mordin has demonstrated that weight only encumbers horses significantly when they are travelling at maximum speed; our equine friends slow considerably to undertake turns and thus weight is a greater issue when horses are racing in a straight line.

The ratings that appear in newspapers and formbook publications are typically adjusted for the weight that horses are set to carry in forthcoming races. Hence, if a horse that is rated 10 lbs clear of the field is carrying a penalty of three lbs in weight relative to the other runners, then the animal's advantage is thought to be only seven lbs. Although the sample that I used to analyse private handicap ratings (see Graph 2) consisted of non-handicaps races, these contests are still riddled with various types of weight penalty and allowance. In conditions races, penalties are allotted on the basis on past performances, such as wins in races over a certain value. Younger horses and fillies generally benefit from a weight allowance that is thought to redress the natural advantage possessed by their older and male peers respectively.

I made no correction to account for the effect of weight when I analysed the relationship of raceform ratings to performance (see Graph 2). Notably, the ratings represent a very sound predictor of performance and profit when weight is completely ignored. In the year 2000, I used a private handicap rating as part of a systematic betting approach. When the flat season was only a month or so old, I realised in a flash that I was not adjusting these ratings for the weights that horses were carrying and I thus set out to do so. Luckily, I indulged my incredulity by testing the effects of making the weight correction on the previous year's results. This procedure decimated the profit that I had shown and hence I resolved not to make any corrections.

I sought to repeat the analysis presented in Graph 2, but with different weight corrections made to account for the burdens. In the first instance, I corrected the ratings for the effects of weight in the normal way (described above). Thereafter, I attempted to make smaller corrections and reduced the rating only by half a pound for every pound of additional weight that a horse bore. I tried various ratios including those above one pound. Thus, I also reduced the ratings by two lbs for every additional pound in weight carried. As predicted, I found that adjusting the ratings for weight in the orthodox fashion weakens the relationship between ratings and performance; the SR% in the case of top-rated animals was not as high when one corrected the ratings for weight (see Graph 3).

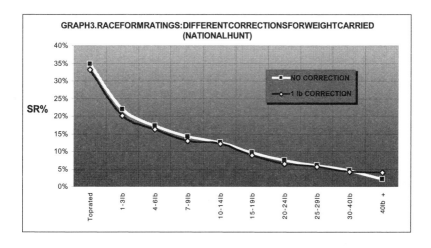

Of course, the laws of physics indicate that additional saddle weight must exert some negative effect on racehorse performance. However, it is clear that this effect is currently over-estimated by those who compile handicaps. My research indicates that the optimal level of correction lies between 0.25 and 0.50 lbs. In other words, the effects of weight are currently over-estimated by a factor of between 2 and 4.

The real problem is not the correction that is made to the ratings of runners in a forthcoming race; that can easily be eliminated or reversed. The difficulty lies in the fact that weight corrections have been used all the way through the process of compiling the ratings. Although I do not disagree in principle with a rating system that evaluates the performances of horses based on the distances they win and lose by, I do not think that such a system should be scaled by weight. The effects of weight should be accounted for and analysed separately. Unfortunately, speed ratings are also confounded by weight in the same manner as handicap ratings; i.e., a speed figure is adjusted to account for the weight that a horse is set to carry relative to the other runners in a race.

There are further drawbacks associated with quantifying the effects of weight. Firstly, the burden a horse must bear is determined by various factors: the weight of the jockey, the weight of the horse's tack and saddle, and also the lead weight carried in the saddlecloth. The vigorous exertions of the jockey provide assistance to the muscular contractions of the galloping horse. Whereas a good jockey is well balanced and assists the horse, saddle weight is dead and merely encumbers the animal. Hence, the proportion of the jockey's weight to the dead weight in the saddlecloth is a significant consideration.

The second issue regarding weight is that horses vary greatly in their stature and physique. The skeletal frame, bodyweight, galloping style, and muscularity of a horse will all influence its suitability for bearing loads. Hence, twelve stones on the back of a frail and delicate horse may exert a far greater effect than the same weight borne by a broad, muscular type of steed. Similarly, it would be a fallacy to think that all human athletes have the same weight-bearing capabilities. For example, Dwaine Chambers, the former British 100m champion, was built like the proverbial brick outhouse whereas other successful sprinters such as America's Tim Montgomery are wiry and lean. The difference in physique between Montgomery and Chambers may have had something to do with the fact that one of them was on everything but roller skates. Nevertheless, the two men would obviously react very differently to an extra weight burden and the same principle is true of horses. However, weight is allotted in the same way to each horse regardless of its physical characteristics.

Ratings Scales: A Conclusion

Despite all of their limitations, rating scales have obvious utility and they provide a useful shortcut for individuals who are getting to grips with racing. Ability ratings also constitute a very powerful variable for use in systematic betting approaches. Indeed, of all the different statistical information that exists about a given horse, ratings are typically the most significant.

Whereas handicap marks cannot always be used to identify the likely winner of a race, they can serve to point out horses that are highly likely to lose. In this way, ratings function as a 'wide-filter', thus providing a fast means of narrowing down a field of runners. Whether one is spending time analysing form before a race or entering data into a computer programme, it certainly helps to eliminate half the field in one fell swoop. However, the more expert and knowledgeable a backer becomes, the less likely she is to depend on the numerical rating attributed to a horse and the more likely she is to consider the various moderating factors that affect racehorse performance. In particular, the concept of speed ratings has yet to be fully exploited in British betting.

Due to the nature of the betting market, it is essential to hold opinions that do not simply mirror those of the betting public. Unfortunately, the odds-compilers pay close attention to ability ratings when forming a market, so the relative ability of the horses in question is normally accounted for in the prices that are on offer. Nevertheless, there are certainly instances when this is not the case. Indeed, the principle behind some of my best results has been to identify instances when the betting public underestimates a horse with proven recent form.

CHAPTER 10
Handicap Races

The domain of handicap racing is the ideal testing ground for theories regarding the effects of weight. I decided to analyse the performance of runners carrying varying amounts of weight and the returns derived from backing them. The principle I adopted was similar to the one that I used when analysing ratings in that the top-weight in each race was given a score of '0'. Therefore, a horse that was burdened by two stones less than the top-weight was given a score of '28' (2 stones = 28 lbs). Handicaps also feature incidental weight advantages such as those given to apprentice jockeys. However, I found that such allowances made little difference to the outcome of my analyses, which are based on the actual weight carried by each runner. In Graph 4, I have presented the relationship between weight borne, profit, and SR% for flat racing.

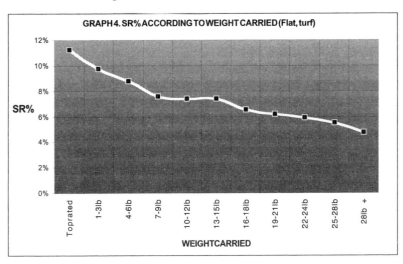

Clearly, the extra weight that is carried by the more able runners does not impede their performance in the way that it is supposed to. Profit is another issue entirely, for it appears that the prices that are on offer in respect of the better horses (who bear the heavier weights) take into account their superior ability. Indeed, the only trend that I discovered was that horses bearing lower weights (below 10st 8lb) in National Hunt racing appear to offer the smallest losses

74 Against the Odds

(variable stakes loss = -8p). Many studies have reported findings that confirm the supremacy of horses carrying the higher weights. Furthermore, one often encounters the folk wisdom: "well it's carrying the heaviest weight because it's the best horse in the race." Also, those who pedal racing systems often enthusiastically discuss the prospects of following top-weights combined with other selection criteria. All of these factors may have combined to influence the shape of the betting market in handicap races. The mediocre return derived from backing topweights proves that making a profit does not necessarily mean routinely picking the horse which is most likely to win. As a backer in search of financial gain, you are at the mercy of the market.

The official handicap marks are assessed on a weekly basis and may be revised to account for recent performances. The handicapper will raise the mark of a horse that has won or is considered to have performed well. A horse climbing the handicap scale will either carry a heavier weight against similar rivals on the next occasion that it races or face tougher competition. Conversely, when a horse fails to make the frame, its mark is reduced until it has a chance to be competitive. Thus, competitive racing is the ultimate objective of the handicapper and the canon of his merit. With this in mind, I sought to investigate the profit returned by runners that had risen or fallen in the handicap. There is a trend that links raised handicap marks with improved performance, i.e., horses whose handicap marks have been increased do win more frequently than those whose marks have been lowered. However, the market accounts for this trend and there appears to be no wholesale advantage for the backer to exploit. In fact, rather than considering any increase or decrease in handicap mark, it is far more relevant to ask if the animal is running in a higher or lower grade than in its previous race; a subject I investigate in Chapter 19.

I sought trends relating to the effects of weight at different race distances. Unexpectedly, the horses burdened by higher weights outperformed those bearing lower weights by the same degree regardless of distance. In National Hunt racing, a minor trend emerged which suggested that large weights are more difficult to bear at longer distances. This pattern did not exert a noticeable effect on performance (SR %) but it did impact upon betting returns. In races of 3m 2f and further, laying heavily-weighted runners returned a profit. I isolated runners bearing a weight that was within 3lb of the topweight in each race; 164 runners who met this criterion started at odds of less than 2/1. If you had laid each one to lose £100 then a profit of £2132 would have been collected.

Anecdotally, the Grand National provides the ideal example of a long-distance jump race in which heavily-weighted runners struggle. Whereas many horses carrying over 11 stones or more have made the frame in the famous race, there normally appears to be at least one less-encumbered runner too good for the classier types. If we ignore 2005, we have to trawl back towards glorious specimens like Red Rum in order to uncover exceptions to this rule. On the flat, I also found evidence that topweights struggle in longer-distance contests. In races run over two miles or more, the 1600 runners bearing 9 stones 6 lb or less returned a variable stakes loss of only 6p (per £ staked) which was set against a loss of 27p for those weighted within 3 lb of the topweight.

As is the case with humans, fillies and mares are physically smaller and lighter than their male counterparts. I chose to investigate any differences between the weight-bearing capabilities of the two sexes. In National Hunt racing, I found that female topweights won only 14.6% of their races, which compares to a figure of 16.1% for male topweights. I then searched for females that were set to carry a weight that was within three lbs of the topweight in each race. I found 276 such runners that were sent off at prices below 3/1. To have laid each one to lose £100 would have resulted in an overall profit of £2,646. I could not find an equivalent sex difference in flat racing. A possible reason for this finding is that runners on the flat generally carry between 8 and 10 stones whereas their jumping cousins hump between 10 and 12 stones over obstacles.

Due to their relatively large fields and competitive nature I find that handicap races are inherently less predictable than their non-handicap counterparts. Nevertheless, most successful backers that I have encountered actually favour handicaps. The complexity of the form can provide more opportunities for experienced bettors to gain a foothold and establish an edge over less methodical gamblers. The amount of effort that bookmakers expend on promoting handicaps (sponsorship, promotion, advance prices) suggests that these races generate a high level of profit for them. Hence, it follows that the betting public does not fare well in handicaps.

There are several good reasons to explain the ambiguity of handicap form. Firstly, the essential nature of the handicap system functions to punish ability: There is a huge incentive for those connected with horses (i.e., owners and trainers) to ensure that a horse performs poorly in order to achieve a low handicap mark which can then be exploited. The simplest method to vouchsafe a weak run is to enter a horse in a race that confounds the animal's preferences. For example, envisage a gelding horse that has shown a distinct preference for soft ground. The trainer need only enter the horse in a series of races on firm ground during the summer to yield a string of poor performances. Consequently, a low handicap mark will enable the horse to display an unexpected improvement when he encounters his preferred soft surface again in the autumn. There are far more subtle ways of achieving the same result. For example, certain horses require longer recovery periods in between races than others. If one such horse is given a series of races in quick succession followed by a recuperation period to enable proper recovery then a low handicap mark and inflated odds could be exploited for financial gain. Whereas such practices are 'legitimate,' others contravene the rules of racing. For example, trainers have been known to order jockeys to stop or "stuff" horses in order to prevent them from running to their true potential. Of course, one could also ensure a gambling opportunity in a non-handicap race by preventing a horse from showing its true ability in public. However, handicaps by their very nature are particularly conducive to the duplicitous practices described above; in order to win it is necessary to beat the handicapper.

THE RECLASSIFICATION OF HANDICAPS

In response to mounting criticism of handicaps, the BHB adopted a new race classification structure on the flat in September 2004. Previously there were too many handicap bands without a clear enough distinction between them in terms of prize money. Consequently, this poorly-defined structure has been simplified into five bands (see Table 2 on page 35), each with its own discrete prize money bracket. For example, Class 2 handicaps are worth between £10,000 and £20,000 and must be contested by runners that are rated between 71 and 85. Another factor that discouraged competitive racing was the broad weight-range of most handicaps. Under the old system, it was possible for a horse to win the same prize money as another that was rated 30 lbs higher. In order to correct this imbalance, the weight differential of handicaps has been restricted to a narrower band of between 10 and 15 lbs. One exception to this rule is that valuable 'heritage' handicaps such as the Lincoln and Cesarewitch will retain their broad weight differentials. The implication is that the prior structure was an invitation to run horses other than on their merits. It is hoped that the changes will deliver a true meritocracy in which ability will be better rewarded.

HANDICAPS: A CONCLUSION

When considering the runners in a forthcoming race, it is common practice among successful backers to whittle the field down to a small number of possible winners that can then be subjected to scrutiny. Handicaps often produce large and competitive fields. Such a proliferation of potential victors can easily befog the mind of even the most adroit backer. The competitive nature of handicaps is not determined by the weight differential but by the fact that horses of similar ability are brought together. Although the effect of weight is quite minimal, it does appear to further confuse the outcome. Even within the handicap sphere there are variants which are thought to be particularly opaque from the backer's point of view. For instance, it is often remarked that sprint handicappers take it in turns to win their races. The equivalent contest under National Hunt rules would be the two mile handicap hurdle. David Ashforth once wrote that with three hours of hard work one

The Cesarewitch, one of the heritage handicaps

might hope to narrow down the field in such a race to 20 possibles!

Personally, I seldom bet in handicaps. Form is never what it appears to be and my methodical approaches are far more applicable to the relatively ordered world of non-handicaps. I anticipate that this scruple is likely to be eroded somewhat following the changes to flat racing's classification system. My expectation is that the revised structure will render handicaps a more viable betting medium. Nevertheless, I would still advise caution. Handicaps can prove to be the graveyard of the inexperienced backer. Even if you feel sufficiently practised, always regard handicaps and non-handicaps as very distinct entities. I have found that betting approaches transfer very poorly from one arena to the other.

CHAPTER 11

Finishing Positions and Margins of Victory

One of the first contentions I can remember forming about betting was that if two horses were rated equally then you should back the horse that came closest to winning its previous race. The reasoning behind this schoolboy theory was that the chosen animal had demonstrated its ability to compete, albeit in a weaker race than its adversary.

To put this idea to the test I restricted my sample to top-rated horses running on the flat in non-handicaps. It is a point of interest that, although a modest profit followed when backing runners that had won their previous start, the best returns came from supporting horses that had finished well down the field on their previous attempt. For example, using the speed ratings earned on the most recent start, I identified 206 horses that were top-rated yet had finished out of the first nine places. Backing each of these led to a 27p profit (per £ staked) which equated to £5,589 if one had used £100 stakes. If one widens the sample to include all horses rated within 5lb of the top-rated animal then the number of qualifiers increases to 767 yet the profit level remains the same. Hence, the return to £100 stakes was £21,476. Clearly, the selections concerned are horses moving down to a lower class (the subject of Chapter 19). Also, for such respectable profits to have been forthcoming, the betting public at large must have under-estimated the prospects of these runners owing to a poor placing on the most recent start. In most formbooks, a finish worse than ninth is represented by '0', regardless of the actual placing. Possibly this lack of information contributed to the betting patterns that led to the profit I reported. The average price of the selections was 11/2.

In accordance with expectations, the finishing position of a horse in its previous race bears a clear relationship with SR% (see Graph 5). Indeed, an impressive strike rate of over 25% is achieved by horses that had won their preceding start. The results also indicate that horses that finish worse than 7th generally make poor betting propositions on their subsequent starts. As a statistic, the finishing position has numerous disadvantages. It is better to finish second in a field of thirty runners than in a field of three runners, yet both performances appear the same when you glance at the form figures which are printed next to the runners' names in the newspaper. It is possible for a horse to be beaten into second place by thirty lengths while a different animal might finish seventh yet be only a couple of lengths distant from the winner. From a psychological point of view, that '2' or '3' printed next the horse's name in the newspaper is very beguiling. However, we must always want to know more about the manner of a horse's victory or defeat.

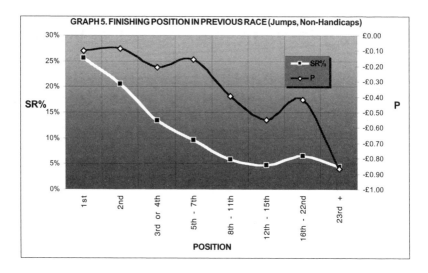

GRAPH 5. FINISHING POSITION IN PREVIOUS RACE (Jumps, Non-Handicaps)

I analysed the performance of horses according to the number of lengths that they were beaten by in their previous run (see Table 9). Of course, the length of the race exerts a large influence on the interpretation of a winning margin: A five length victory would not be regarded as unusual over 2m whereas it would seem quite emphatic over 5f. Rather than convert the margin of victory into lbs, which is difficult to envisage when attempting to consider the results, I simply limited the sample to include only those horses whose previous race was around 1m (between 7.5 and 8.5f).

TABLE 9. AN ANALYSIS OF LENGTHS BEATEN IN PREVIOUS RACE				
(Flat non-hcaps where prev. race was 7.5-8.5f)				
LENGTHS BEATEN BY	SR%	N	P	VSP
0 (WINNERS)	19.3%	755	-£0.04	-£0.05
NOSE	30.6%	36	£0.79	-£0.06
HEAD	34.1%	44	£0.26	£0.13
NECK	24.1%	112	-£0.19	-£0.05
0.5	26.1%	115	£0.14	-£0.02
0.75	31.0%	87	£0.09	£0.11
1	30.4%	102	£0.22	£0.10
1.5 – 2	19.8%	556	-£0.24	-£0.17
2.5 – 4	17.0%	988	-£0.20	-£0.08
4.5 – 6	13.0%	948	-£0.30	-£0.11
7 – 10	10.4%	1647	-£0.19	-£0.08
11 – 15	7.0%	1504	-£0.29	-£0.10
16 – 20	4.8%	930	-£0.56	-£0.14
21 – 30	3.1%	956	-£0.59	-£0.32
31 +	2.3%	560	-£0.72	-£0.38

Predictably, the SR% appears to be inversely proportional to the distance that the horse was beaten by on its last run. However, it is interesting to note that horses which had lost by a narrow margin outperformed winners, both in terms of SR% and profit. A winner may not necessarily have been stretched whereas a narrowly beaten horse would have competed. If one had backed every runner beaten by a length or less from the sample in question then a profit of 13p (per £ staked) would have followed. Alternatively, if each of the 496 selections had carried a £100 stake then a profit of £6,448 would have been banked. This particular trend favouring narrowly beaten runners is not as pronounced in National Hunt racing. Nevertheless, in non-handicaps the 1,564 runners that were beaten by two lengths or less (regardless of race distance) returned a very small profit if backed on their following starts. In National Hunt handicaps, runners that were well beaten (10 lengths or more) on their preceding start made good laying fodder. My sample included 276 such runners that started at less than 2/1. If one had laid each of these to lose £100 then a profit of £3036 would have been the reward.

One generally encounters two opposing schools of thought on the subject of winning distances. A large margin of victory may indicate sheer ability or just a lack of competition. Those who subscribe to the latter view prefer to follow horses that are involved in battling finishes and prevail by the slightest of margins. A performance analysis showed that horses which had won their previous starts by a large margin outperformed those that had achieved a narrow victory. For example, in National Hunt racing, runners that had won by less than a length went on to win 18% of their subsequent races. This strike rate compares to a healthier figure of around 28% in respect of horses that had previously triumphed by 15 lengths or more.

However, there appeared to be scant advantage to the backer in following those horses that had won by a large margin. On the contrary, it appears that backers bet too heavily on runners that had won their previous start by a considerable distance. I found 574 runners that had triumphed by a distance of less than two lengths over 8f. When backed with variable stakes, these selections returned a profit of 3p (per £ staked) on their following starts, whereas the 80 runners that had won by over 4 lengths returned a loss of 35p. In National Hunt racing this trend proved even more pronounced. Indeed, it was profitable to lay short priced (< 2/1) runners that had won non-handicaps by distances of 15 lengths or more. My sample included 234 such horses and if I had laid each one with the usual stake (to lose £100) then the profit would have been £3,907.

A weakness in my analysis is that it only concerns the distance that separated the winner and second-placed finishers. Although a race might be won by ten lengths, it is possible that four runners could dead-heat for second place. On the contrary, all of the finishers might be separated by a distance of 10 lengths. To examine this principle I focused on races with 10 or more runners and considered the distance by which the winner had beaten the 5th placed runner. This analysis yielded very different results. Essentially, winners of races that finish strung out are good betting propositions whereas winners of races that finish with little distance separating the first five provide good laying opportunities. In a sample of National Hunt non-handicaps, the 2,557 winners that had beaten the fifth-placed runner by 20 lengths or more returned a strike rate of 29.2% when next racing and only a slight loss to level stakes. Conversely, in a sample of all National Hunt races, winners that had beaten the fifth-placed horse by less than 10 lengths returned a strike rate of only 17%. Three-hundred and fifty one of these selections were sent off at odds of less than 2/1. If each one had been laid to lose £100 then a profit of £5,124 would have been reaped.

CHAPTER 12

Trainers

If the entire racehorse population was divided randomly between the many training establishments then we would know who the better trainers are. However, the success of a yard depends largely on the quality of horses therein. Nevertheless, the skills and practices of each trainer are idiosyncratic and shape the ability and development of the horses in her care. Trainers prepare their horses for races in markedly different ways. Furthermore, each handler enjoys success with specific types of runners and races. Hence, it is not true to think that the trainer's influence will be fully accounted for by the previous form the horse has shown. There are patterns of results relating to trainers that provide opportunities for the bettor.

Another source of encouragement is the huge public bias towards popular trainers. Most gamblers that you encounter on course or in betting offices are unfamiliar with the peculiar characteristics and form of individual horses. However, the identity of a successful trainer is far more memorable and the inexperienced backer will often bet on the trainer rather than the horse. This bias disturbs the market and can result in favourable prices if one is prepared to refrain from backing horses that are trained by the big potatoes in the racing field.

Trainers provide a very good subject for statistical analysis and consequently form an important consideration when one is adopting a systematic approach to betting. I have always placed great store in considering the trainer of the horse that I am backing (or laying!). What is the trainer's record in this type of contest? How are the trainer's horses performing? This information is very readily available but it is often overlooked by the betting public who are mesmerised by the idolatry that surrounds legendary trainers like Martin Pipe and Aidan O'Brien. Indeed, Kate Fox wrote very perceptively about the role of the trainer in racing society and likened it to that of a shaman in a tribal culture; exulted and beyond censure or reproach. The trainer is far more responsible for the condition and performance of a horse than the jockey, who takes his riding orders from the trainer. However, dissatisfied punters can be heard to yell rancorous abuse at the losing jockey rather than the trainer. When was the last time you saw an embittered punter ripping up a betting slip and muttering to himself, "that b*st*rd Michael Stoute!"

I evaluated the relationship between the trainer's strike rate, the horse's performance, and profit (see Graph 6). The trainer's SR% figures are cumulative, which means that they reflect the trainer's performance over the whole season to date. As expected, the trainer's strike rate is a very potent predictor of both performance and profit. We observe a gradual improvement in returns and SR% as we move across the graph. The curve is quite smooth until we approach the data points that represent runners trained by those with high strike rates (> 20%). Doubtless, these figures represent very small sample sizes that originate from the beginning of the season. For example, a given trainer might be lucky enough to win with five of her first ten runners during a season. However, a strike rate of 50% would be unsustainable over the course of the year. For example, whereas over 21,649 runners in the sample were sent off by handlers with a strike rate in the region of 10-15% at the time of the race, only 401 runners were saddled by trainers with a strike rate of 30-35%.

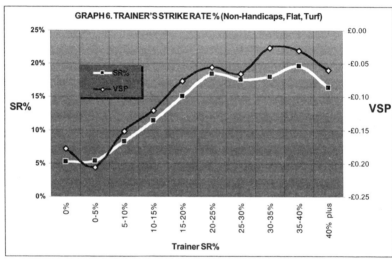

GRAPH 6. TRAINER'S STRIKE RATE % (Non-Handicaps, Flat, Turf)

Martin Pipe

Aidan O'Brien

In order to ascertain under what conditions the trainer's strike rate was an important consideration, I repeated the analysis presented in Graph 6 with data from different types of race. On the flat, I found that the trainer's SR% is a statistic that merits much greater consideration when making a selection in non-handicap races. In the case of National Hunt races, no such distinction applies: Whether betting in handicaps or non-handicaps, runners whose trainer had attained a SR of between 20% and 50% almost yielded a profit. Interestingly, I found that the trainer's strike rate is an especially pertinent statistic to consider when betting in races for young or inexperienced horses (e.g., two-year-olds or three-year-old maidens): Reliable form is at a premium and most of the horses in question are improving rapidly. At this formative stage, a young thoroughbred is particularly dependent on the methods and competencies of his trainer. It is unsurprising then that the trainer's strike rate is a very good predictor of performance and profit in bumpers; the National Hunt equivalent of two-year-old races on the flat. Indeed, a modest profit was made by backing every runner whose trainer had a strike rate of over 25%.

RECENT STRIKE RATES

It is well known that the form of stables ebbs and flows throughout the season. This is a somewhat mysterious phenomenon, which may have various causes. In large stables, horses are prepared for the primary meetings. Smaller stables might aim their better horses at the prizes that fall either too early or late in the season to suit the training patterns of the star performers from more glamorous yards. The condition of the gallops may be affected by bad weather, which is localised and therefore does not affect all stables. Similarly, horses that are trained in the south of the country may take advantage of an earlier spring.

Horses in training live in very close quarters and any viral infection is likely to affect the yard as a whole. As I am writing this, Jonjo O' Neill's yard is in the throes of an infection that will almost certain preclude his string from playing any part in the forthcoming Cheltenham festival. Those who work in stables have cited the influence of psychological factors; the underlying mood of a yard is said to influence the care that horses receive and colour their approach to training. For example, heads can quickly begin to drop if the stable encounters a run of poor results or the trainer treats his staff unfairly. All of the above goes to show that it is not just the trainer's personal strike rate but that of the stable which he manages. Yards with massive strings of horses such as those of Mick Channon or Richard Hannon are very much influenced by the assistant trainers, lads and lasses.

In addition to the trainer's strike rate for the season to date, the racing press and formbooks include a statistic that relates to recent form; the SR% over the previous two weeks. I found that the recent SR% variable did not really offer any improvement over the cumulative statistic and in many cases just yielded more erratic results because of the smaller sample sizes involved. It may be true that the peaks in trainers' form are ephemeral and cannot be measured. It has often been noted that a horse will win on the same afternoon as his stable mate or after a good showing from his yard over the course of a festival meeting. Such spikes of form (or shrewd planning by the trainer) would typically not be revealed by analysis of recent form. Also, it is important to assess a trainer's recent form in the context of what is normal for them; it is obviously not much use comparing Saeed Bin Suroor's form (SR of 25%) with that of Milton Bradley (SR of 6%). Due to these issues, I chose to investigate performance and profit in the light of the trainer's previous ten runners; an approach that yielded some encouraging findings. Take as an example the performance of Sir Michael Stoute's runners (Table 10).

TABLE 10. SIR MICHAEL STOUTE'S RECENT STRIKE RATE				
WINNERS FROM LAST 10 RUNNERS	N	SR%	P	VSP
0	153	17.7%	-£0.18	-£0.11
1	250	20.0%	-£0.10	-£0.13
2	249	21.3%	-£0.11	-£0.02
3	219	24.7%	-£0.16	£0.02
4	74	14.9%	-£0.23	-£0.37
5	64	26.6%	£0.24	£0.24
6	17	23.5%	-£0.24	£0.05

Sir Michael Stoute

By his own standards, the runners which Stoute saddles following a lean series of results produce a low level of profit and a poor strike rate. Curiously, the same applies to horses that he sent out when boasting a strike rate of 40% from his last ten runners. This result appears to be an anomaly that defies the underlying trend. Indeed, backing each of Stoute's runners when he is in particularly good recent form (> 4 winners from his previous 10 runners) leads to a comfortable profit. If one had placed £100 on each of these animals then a profit of around £1,134 would have resulted. One could then no doubt buy a very small share in one of the great man's horses; a hoof or pastern perhaps. The results that follow from this approach are unique to the individual trainer in question and obviously depend on the overall profitability of following runners sent out by the handler in question. For example, Mick Channon places so many horses that it is impossible to discern any clear trends because of all the 'noise' present in the data. On the contrary, John Gosden is an interesting case. When he is on good form (> 3 winners from previous 10 runners), his horses return a good profit. I found 208 such examples in my sample and a £100 stake on each of these yielded a profit of £3,581; enough to keep a horse in training for three months or so.

John Gosden

The really interesting thing about Gosden's record is that he exemplifies a phenomenon that I've come to know as bottoming. The argument goes that a trainer's form changes throughout the season in a wave-like pattern. Hence, a peak must inevitably be followed by a trough and vice versa. The worry is that once a peak has been identified, then it will already have gone and is likely to be followed in quick succession by a lean period. The opposite also applies, in that a famine is normally followed by a feast, so to speak. In the case of John Gosden, this is particularly so. Within the period of my sample he saddled 118 horses at a point when his last ten runners had lost. These selections returned a pleasing 24% strike rate (compared to an 18% SR for other runners) and a fantastic level of profit (76p per £ staked). Despite the relatively small sample size, we can conclude that John Gosden is clearly a man to watch in an apparently lean spell. In fact, if you had backed each of the 118 horses in question with a £100 stake, the result would have improved your bank balance to the tune of £8,968. That would buy you a lot of Panamas (hats or cigars but no canal).

In National Hunt racing, profit can readily be generated by examining the recent performance of trainers. For example, the champion trainer Martin Pipe sent off 418 horses at a time when his strike rate was zero from his previous ten runners. These runners performed relatively poorly (SR = 14.8%) and the level stakes loss was huge (37p per £ staked). Contrast this with the runners that the Nicholashayne handler sent out when his strike rate was five or more (from previous ten runners). The 200 runners in question won 34.6% of their races. If you had backed them all to a £100 stake then the profit would have been £13,244 (66.2p per £ staked).

Interesting results can be uncovered if we whittle down the frame of the analysis still further from the previous ten runs to five. John Dunlop is a fine example in this context. When his strike rate was zero (from previous 5 runs), his runners performed poorly (SR = 13%; 25p variable stakes loss). Whereas, when his recent strike rate was two or more, his horses ran well (SR = 23%) and backing them led to a variable stakes profit of 11p (per £ staked). The above demonstrates the importance of considering each trainer's idiosyncrasies. Nevertheless, it is still possible to abstract a general trend that can be used to generate profit. When the trainer's strike rate is high (3 or more winners from previous 10 runners) then performance is good (SR = 24%) and, when a variable stake is used, a slight profit is achieved.

Contrast this result with the performance of runners whose trainer is experiencing a lean spell (10 consecutive losers). In such cases, the strike rate is closer to 11% and the betting return is so poor that laying is the preferable option. I found 588 odds-on favourites in my sample whose trainers were on a doughnut (10 consecutive losers). If one had laid each of these selections to lose £100 then a profit of £14,112 would have been collected (24p per £ staked). I should mention that the above results related to flat non-handicaps and I only included runners whose trainers had fielded ten or more horses inside the previous month.

It is important to look beyond the statistics to a certain extent. Over a period as short as fourteen days, the trainer's performance can be skewed by just a couple of soft results such as horses that are thrown in to weak races. When seen in this light, it seems crude to express the performance of a trainer purely in terms of a wins-to-runs ratio. A more comprehensive approach would be to consider the performance of a trainer's horses against expectations using a rating scale.

The 'runs to form' percentage presented in the *Racing Post* newspaper is a statistic that describes how many of a trainer's recent runners have run within a certain margin of their predicted performance rating. I decided to take this approach a step further by investigating the utility of compiling a rating to assess how each trainer's horses were running in relation to expectations. For example, would it pay to follow trainers whose horses were generally running ten lbs better than on their previous starts? Although this technique sounded potentially fruitful I have to conclude that it was notoriously difficult to action. Differences in the recent performances of a trainer's runners seem to be strongly affected by factors such as the placing of horses in the big races that fill the cards in festival meetings etc. Nevertheless, my results were not entirely discouraging.

Trainers whose horses were running (on average) ten lbs better than expected produced a small profit to level stakes and the strike rate was 16.2% This contrasts with a strike rate of only 12.3% in respect of horses that were fielded by trainers whose runners were performing ten lbs worse than expected. I found a clearer pattern in the case of individual trainers. For example, when Nicky Henderson's horses were generally performing at least 4 lb better than expected, a profit of 21p (per £ staked) was returned by backing his runners. If one had backed the 251 selections in my sample that met this criterion with the usual £100 stake then a profit of £5,552 would have resulted. However, when Henderson's runners were performing beneath expectations by at least 4lb, a 30p loss was shown; 108 of these selections started at odds of less than 2/1. If one had laid them all to lose £100 then an overall profit of £2,376 would have shown.

TRAINERS' CHARACTERISTICS

When you reach the stage that you are familiar with the recent performances of a given trainer's runners without having to be reminded, then you are developing an excellent 'feel' for the sport. Obviously, it is not practical or desirable to attempt to develop an in-depth knowledge of every stable's traits and characteristic patterns. Nevertheless, it is a good idea to be familiar with the operations of a handful of trainers so that you can attune yourself to good betting opportunities. It is particularly useful if the knowledge you develop is not well known to the betting public. Familiarity with Saeed Bin Suroor's string and their recent performances is the province of many armchair racing enthusiasts and is consequently unlikely to provide you with an edge.

I aim to acquaint myself with Irish jumps form prior to the Cheltenham festival. In particular, I focus on two or three handlers and keep tabs with their performances in the major Irish meetings prior to March. This endeavour requires surprisingly little effort and I feel it gives me a really good platform to approach the Festival form, especially as Irish-trained horses are proving increasingly successful at the meeting. It is true that anyone who picks up the Racing Post during the Festival can also assess the results of Irish races. However, I have benefited from an opportunity to appraise the peculiarities and nuances of the form rather than merely skimming through a compressed retrospective account. There is one caveat that I bear in mind when focussing on the runners of a specific trainer. I try hard not to lose my objectivity and allow myself to become affiliated to a specific stable (or horse). It is really important not to favour a selection simply because it's the only one you really know about.

A further approach that I tested was to develop trainers' strike rates for specific types of races; for example, only considering a trainer's two-year-old runners when determining his strike rate. I applied this method to flat horses racing after a rest of two months or more. In order to develop a specific strike rate for each trainer, I considered all his runners from the previous season that met the criterion. I found that, in the 400 cases that this specific strike rate was over 25%, a slight profit was returned to variable stakes. Hence, refining the strike rate statistic in this way can lead to slight improvements over statistics that include all of a trainer's runners.

While it is possible to analyse the performances of each trainer across various types of race, I have refrained from doing so as there are too many people practising this art already. Personally, I have never enthused about endlessly protracted analyses of each trainer's results in different types of races and at different tracks. My objections basically stem from the smallness of the sample sizes involved. It is all very well to know that Martin Pipe's novice chasers excel in 2m 4f events at Fontwell, but there may have only been a handful of qualifiers in the last three years and the pattern could be subject to rapid swings. A more valid approach would be to investigate the performance of each trainer with certain types of runners. In so doing, the sample size would remain large enough to draw some tentative conclusions. Because a trainer's performance and idiosyncrasies change over time, I chose to consider the return in each separate year of my sample. Of course, the ideal would be to pinpoint a trainer whose runners produce a consistent profit year on year when backed under specific conditions. Sadly, this hardly ever happens. Nevertheless, it is important to know that the profit generated over a five-year period is not entirely attributable to the first year of the sample.

I analysed the returns from following National Hunt trainers when fielding specific types of runners (e.g., runners returning after a short or long absence, juveniles, runners at Cheltenham etc.). A selection of these results is displayed in Table 11, and while there are no obvious 'retirement plans' in evidence there are certainly indications of where the respective trainers' competencies lie. The profit figures listed for each season in the sample are running totals and thus indicate profit to date *at that time*. For example, the total profit derived from backing Nicky Henderson's runners when they returned to the racecourse after less than 14 days was 15p (per £ staked) up to and including the 2002-2003 season. A slight improvement was shown in the next season; the overall profit for the five-year period rose to 19p.

TABLE 11. RETURNS FROM BACKING THE RUNNERS OF National Hunt TRAINERS									
				ROLLING PROFIT (P) AT EACH SEASON'S END					
TYPE OF RUNNER	TRAINER	N	SR	VSP	2000	2001	2002	2003	2004
LESS THAN	PAUL NICHOLLS	268	26.9%	£0.34	£0.00	-£0.01	£0.00	-£0.01	£0.00
14 DAYS REST	NICKY HENDERSON	98	25.5%	£0.40	£0.00	-£0.29	£0.00	£0.15	£0.19
	CHARLIE MANN	135	18.5%	£0.30	£0.00	£0.26	£0.36	£0.23	£0.41
	M TODHUNTER	84	17.9%	£0.41	-£0.22	-£0.24	-£0.08	£0.13	£0.13
MORE THAN	J HOWARD JOHNSON	212	18.4%	£0.41	£0.25	£0.68	£0.30	£0.26	£0.24
100 DAYS REST	C EGERTON	105	24.8%	£0.43	£0.51	£0.12	£0.19	£0.17	£0.05
	P BOWEN	173	17.9%	£0.59	£0.02	-£0.17	-£0.26	£0.19	£0.21
HORSES 6YO AND YOUNGER	N G RICHARDS	431	22.0%	£0.42	£0.09	-£0.06	-£0.08	£0.06	£0.05
RUNNERS AT CHELTENHAM	JONJO O'NEILL	134	16.1%	£0.40	£2.68	£1.25	£0.50	£0.57	£0.56

A CHANGE OF TRAINER

An interesting area for analysis is the performance of horses after a change of trainer. The longer you spend around racehorses the more you understand the potency of psychological factors in determining their performances. A new environment and the exposure to different methods can spark a sudden shift in a horse's attitude. This is especially so in the case of younger horses that are promoted to elite stables when they show signs of ability. I examined the returns derived from backing young (< 9 years) National Hunt horses following a change of handler. I located 1,184 such runners during the period of my sample (SR = 14.2%). The selections returned a healthy profit of 23p (per £ staked), a figure that was boosted to 29p (VSP = 34p) if one focussed on the 205 animals aged under six. If one had simply backed every jumps horse under the age of nine following a change of trainer with a £100 stake then a profit of £26,841 would have been earned. Interestingly, the 500 older runners (>8 years) in my sample that had been moved to a different stable returned a significant loss. It appears that, after a certain point in their careers, horses generally change stable due to worsening performance. An analogy might be drawn with footballers approaching their mid-thirties who are transferred from premiership heavyweights to smaller clubs.

The backer Sydney Harris, suggested strongly in his 2003 book that the move from one stable to another is sometimes used to throw the scent away from a betting coup; the "change in surroundings" being a perfect alibi to explain a performance that is largely unpredicted by the betting public and media. Such an abrupt upturn in form would normally provoke suspicions. Some weight is lent to this provocative theory by the fact that the average SP of such winners is around 8/1. This figure suggests that the runners in question are not particularly favoured in the betting market and explains why it is profitable to follow them; most other backers ignore them.

The potential for physical development in the thoroughbred is exceptional and it is the trainer who crafts and shapes the raw substance of each horse. Without the appropriate training, a potential classic winner would struggle to win a race of any description. Owing to the efforts of institutions such as the international equine institute in Limerick and the burgeoning knowledge base within the industry itself, ever more advanced techniques are being made available to handlers. This progressive climate should reward bettors who pay close attention to the role of the trainer. Indeed, identifying the circumstances under which each trainer's string performs well leads to a significant betting edge not least because such trends often pinpoint winners that have not shown particularly good public form.

Jockeys CHAPTER 13

The jockey is one of the least relevant considerations for the serious backer. Gamblers will routinely blame the jockey when their uninspired selections inevitably trail in behind the rest. However, in truth, good jockeys cannot win without good horses although poor riding can certainly squander a winning chance. There are exceptions to this precept; the legendary horsemanship of Tony McCoy appears to make the difference between victory and defeat in some instances. Jockeys do not affect the performance of horses to the same extent that trainers do. However, this does not stop the betting public from placing their greatest faith in the top riders; a bias that can create opportunities for the shrewd bettor.

Tony McCoy

"When he wins, we lose. His horses' names appear on millions of betting slips purely because he is riding them. Thousands back McCoy blind" **Mike Dillon, Ladbrokes**

How do you discern the ability of a jockey? With difficulty; a jockey's performance in terms of SR% is largely dependent on the stature of the trainer for whom he normally rides. Tony McCoy's awesome reputation was built on the quality and quantity of runners provided by champion trainer Martin Pipe. Success bred success: The reputation that the mercurial Irishman earned from riding Pipe's horses enabled him to acquire very promising rides from other trainers to supplement his wining total. As was the case with his successor Timmy Murphy, McCoy clearly earned the right to ride for the champion trainer. But for other jockeys, the opportunity to regularly ride the more able horses may not be forthcoming. In the same way that George Best never saw the world cup finals because of the relative weakness of the Northern Irish national football team, the ability of some jockeys is never recognised.

It has been suggested that if one analysed the performance of jockeys riding top-rated horses then the results would not be skewed by the ability of the horses. The only pitfall with this analysis is that elite jockeys may be booked to ride top-rated horses that are likely to win for reasons besides their rating. Nevertheless, I investigated the performance of top-rated flat horses in non-handicaps according to the SR% of the jockey in the saddle.

As with my other analyses, the status of 'top-rated' was assigned by comparing the Raceform handicap ratings earned by each runner in its previous race (within the same season). In order to compile a jockey's strike rate I considered his performance in the previous 30 days. I excluded any jockey that had ridden less than 10 runners within this time. The results indicated that jockeyship may influence the performances of top-rated horses. However, the trend that I uncovered was not particularly pronounced. As long as the jockey's strike rate was above 5% then a marginal profit followed from backing top-rated horses (as is the case for all top-rated runners). On the relatively rare occasions that a top-rated horse was ridden by a jockey whose strike rate was zero then a heavy loss was returned. I found 108 odds-on favourites that were top-rated yet ridden by jockeys with a 0% strike rate. These selections returned a comfortable profit of 23p (per £ staked) when laid.

An intelligent answer to the problem of assessing the relative merits of jockeys is to compare different riders' performances on the same horse. This method has elaborated into a whole system of ratings, which are produced twice-yearly by a company known as Racing Research. Despite the utility of these ratings, there is one residual issue that could marginally skew the results: When a horse has been prepared for a big performance (possibly its most important of the season) and a jockey is required, it is more likely that a rider of high standing will be booked. Hence, improvement will be due because the horse would have been trained with the big race in mind. Consequently, the comparison will always work in favour of the jockey taking the ride for the more valuable race.

When a horse from a smaller stable is entered in a prestigious race, the owner(s) generally favour the booking of a well-known jockey, should one be available. Indeed, the booking of a jockey for a spare ride is related to the connections' expectations of how the horse will perform. A ride on an unpromising runner with little chance of victory is less likely to be claimed by a jockey who is seeking every winner he can find to compete in the jockey's championship. Conversely, a potent clue that can advertise the connections' confidence in an apparently mediocre runner is the booking of an experienced jockey. Of course, the circumstances surrounding jockey changes do not always relate to the booking of a fashionable rider. For example, a horse might have changed stables or the established jockey could be unavailable through injury, suspension, or a prior commitment to a different ride.

In fact, after conducting several analyses I decided to ignore the possibility that the booking of a successful jockey might coincide with an expected upturn in form. This was because I found that, following a change of jockey, horses that are raced in a higher grade than on their previous start do not necessarily perform any better in terms of speed ratings. I assessed the average amount of improvement (in lbs) shown by horses following a change of jockey. The results for individual National Hunt jockeys are presented in Table 12, which is equivalent to a 'league table' of jockeys' performance in two columns.

TABLE 12. AVERAGE IMPROVEMENT IN LBS FOR National Hunt JOCKEYS FOLLOWING A JOCKEY CHANGE (FIGURE IN BRACKETS IS THE NUMBER OF RUNS)			
L A Hurley (55)	9.01	B J Geraghty (351)	1.08
R Walsh (365)	6.71	J Culloty (137)	1.04
G T Hutchinson (101)	5.45	B Fenton (108)	0.96
G Lee (160)	5.08	M Foley (76)	0.91
W Hutchinson (50)	4.86	K A Kelly (104)	0.88
A P McCoy (339)	4.75	R Thornton (152)	0.75
R Garritty (54)	4.23	M Bradburne (106)	0.74
P Carberry (275)	3.94	A Ross (62)	0.58
J Mogford (74)	3.78	J A McCarthy (87)	0.46
D R Dennis (95)	3.68	K Whelan (69)	0.32
N Fehily (86)	3.47	J E Moore (74)	0.27
A Thornton (185)	3.29	J P Elliott (51)	0.25
K Hadnett (72)	3.15	J P McNamara (114)	0.22
J M Maguire (53)	3.11	P Aspell (99)	0.21
P J Brennan (50)	2.98	A Dobbin (216)	0.07
L Aspell (118)	2.74	T Scudamore (141)	0.00
I J Power (54)	2.72	R McGrath (138)	-0.11
D Elsworth (90)	2.71	D J Casey (261)	-0.27
R Johnson (377)	2.62	J R Barry (141)	-0.44
R Geraghty (98)	2.57	D O'Meara (66)	-0.59
D Crosse (68)	2.51	W Marston (134)	-0.91
A Dempsey (90)	2.41	N P Mulholland (88)	-0.95
J Crowley (95)	2.38	T P Treacy (93)	-1.11
J L Cullen (146)	2.35	L Cooper (79)	-1.11
D J Howard (78)	2.27	B J Crowley (66)	-1.21
T J Murphy (269)	2.06	N Williamson (289)	-1.24
P A Carberry (87)	1.75	C Llewellyn (116)	-1.66
M D Grant (59)	1.73	T Doyle (112)	-1.69
D N Russell (103)	1.73	P Moloney (146)	-1.71
F King (61)	1.69	L Vickers (53)	-1.87
B Harding (119)	1.65	G Cotter (182)	-2.61
R P McNally (58)	1.41	B Hitchcott (82)	-2.94
H Oliver (89)	1.39	C O'Dwyer (157)	-3.08
B M Cash (94)	1.35	J Tizzard (136)	-3.21
S Durack (144)	1.29	R Greene (151)	-3.49
P Flynn (126)	1.21	M A Fitzgerald (154)	-4.66
S G McDermott (57)	1.18		

The table indicates that when riders were 'jocked-off' by Tony McCoy (near the top of the first column), the runners that he rode performed, on average, nearly five lbs better than on their previous starts. The appearance of certain jockeys in the upper reaches of the table may be due to the small sample sizes in respect of these riders. However, amongst the more seasoned contenders it is clear that Ruby Walsh, Tony McCoy, Russ Garritty, Paul Carberry, and Graham Lee are all riders who impart a lot of improvement to their rides. The neutral point of the table is Tom Scudamore (second column): When he assumed a ride from another jockey, his mounts earned a rating equivalent to that achieved in the preceding race. Of course, this figure is an average. It might be that half such runners improved by 20 lbs whereas the other half ran 20 lbs worse; but this is exceedingly unlikely. Indeed, it beggars belief that a jockey would influence the performance of a horse by more than 20 lbs (equivalent to around 12 lengths in a race over three miles). With this in mind, I repeated the above analysis excluding runners that had performed 10 lbs better or worse than on their previous starts. I reasoned that big improvements or decrements in performance were unlikely to be a result of horsemanship. The results of this restricted analysis appear in Table 13.

TABLE 13. AVERAGE IMPROVEMENT IN LBS FOR National Hunt JOCKEYS FOLLOWING A JOCKEY CHANGE (restricted to a maximum 10 lbs difference between the two runs)			
M D Grant (37)	2.22	D N Russell (52)	0.77
S Durack (69)	2.14	J Crowley (44)	0.66
M Bradburne (56)	1.68	J R Barry (66)	0.64
K A Kelly (60)	1.67	P Flynn (66)	0.56
P Carberry (137)	1.55	C F Swan (51)	0.55
D R Dennis (44)	1.55	P Moloney (64)	0.55
L Aspell (49)	1.53	A Maguire (55)	0.42
R Walsh (167)	1.29	J P McNamara (49)	0.39
R Thornton (60)	1.27	M A Fitzgerald (65)	0.35
G T Hutchinson (43)	1.21	M Foley (36)	0.31
J Culloty (67)	1.12	A Thornton (89)	0.26
G Lee (67)	1.11	C Llewellyn (49)	0.22
R McGrath (57)	1.09	P Aspell (46)	0.22
D J Howard (40)	1.03	G Cotter (93)	0.11
J L Cullen (58)	1.02	N Williamson (137)	0.09
D Elsworth (41)	1.01	T Scudamore (74)	0.01
T J Murphy (138)	0.99	R Greene (69)	-0.26
B J Geraghty (180)	0.97	B Fenton (61)	-0.33
A Dempsey (48)	0.96	W Marston (55)	-0.58
R Johnson (190)	0.92	B Harding (47)	-0.64
A P McCoy (168)	0.88	T P Treacy (43)	-0.67
D J Casey (111)	0.86	R M Power (42)	-0.71
A Dobbin (99)	0.82	J Tizzard (63)	-0.73
L Cooper (42)	0.79	C O'Dwyer (65)	-1.02

Despite some subtle reshuffling, the order is still broadly similar to that which emerged from the unrestricted analysis (See Table 12). Once again, Ruby Walsh and Paul Carberry feature towards the top of the table. It is apparent that horses generally improve when ridden by a different jockey as relatively few jockeys are in the red (e.g., Rodi Greene and the riders beneath). Following the removal of runners that had improved or worsened by 10 lbs or more, Mick Fitzgerald has improved from last place to the middle of the table. This finding indicates that he got on several horses that experienced large dips in form. It is important to emphasise that the jockeys colonising the nether regions of the table are not necessarily weaker horsemen in a general sense. It might be that riders such as Joe Tizzard take longer to acquaint themselves with a horse and develop a winning partnership. Nevertheless, the data used for the above analyses does include runners that have been ridden by the jockey in question before, just not in the previous race. There may also be circumstances that lead a certain rider to be newly paired with runners that are not well prepared to race, a factor that is more attributable to the horse's trainer.

Ruby Walsh   **Paul Carberry**

Knowing whether a horse is likely to run well following a change of jockey is interesting enough, but what does this tell us regarding profit? I analysed all runners that were paired with a different rider (when compared to the previous race) and sought trends relating to profit. A selection of the results is displayed in Table 14 on the following page.

TABLE 14. PERFORMANCE OF National Hunt JOCKEYS FOLLOWING A CHANGE OF RIDER			
JOCKEY	N	SR%	P
C F Swan	159	15.1%	-£0.22
D Elsworth	145	15.2%	-£0.18
Richard Guest	118	19.5%	-£0.16
B J Geraghty	613	15.3%	-£0.13
A P McCoy	556	25.5%	-£0.07
P Carberry	454	20.3%	£0.07
R Johnson	619	19.1%	£0.08
R Walsh	559	19.0%	£0.10
P J Brennan	93	15.1%	£0.24
D R Dennis	174	16.1%	£0.29
L Aspell	238	16.0%	£0.32
W Hutchinson	97	17.5%	£0.58
L Cummins	74	16.2%	£0.95

It is clear that backing jockeys who have been shown to produce improvement from a horse can lead to profit. For example, runners that have been newly paired with either Paul Carberry or Ruby Walsh produce performances several lbs better than on their previous starts (see Tables 12 & 13). It comes as no shock then that to back the mounts of Carberry and Walsh under these circumstances leads to a comfortable profit. This principle is not unilateral; when Tony McCoy assumes a ride from another jockey the marked improvement in performance does not translate into profit. In fact, McCoy provides a classic example of a jockey who is followed too slavishly by the betting public when claiming a ride. Although his strike rate for such rides is a very comfortable 25.5%, the selections return a loss of 7p (per £ staked). Perhaps the most impressive finding relates to Leighton Aspell. If you had backed Aspell with a £100 stake on each of the 238 occasions that he took on a ride from another jockey then you would have been smiling all the way to the bank; the profit was £7,616.

Under certain circumstances, it is profitable to simply back all horses that are paired with a different rider when compared to the previous start. The key is to look for runners that have a strong chance according to form in better quality races. For example, I pinpointed 528 top-rated horses with a new jockey booking in National Hunt races above Class E. If each of these runners had carried the usual £100 stake then the profit would have totalled £17,156 (33p per £ staked). A high strike-rate of around 43% led to a consistent flow of winners.

Until they gain a full professional licence, apprentice (flat) and conditional (jumps) jockeys claim an allowance in terms of a weight advantage over their fully-fledged counterparts. Apprentices claim seven lbs until they have won 20 races, thereafter five lbs until they have won 50 races, and finally three lbs until they have won 95 races, at which point they are eligible to apply for a full professional licence. Conditional jockeys racing under National Hunt rules lose their seven, five, and three pound claims after they have won 15, 35, and 65 races respectively. It will not surprise you to learn that I think the weight advantage fairly irrelevant. Nevertheless, an apprentice's weight claim may prompt a trainer to put up an inexperienced jockey on a heavily-weighted runner in a handicap; a tactic that

In the first edition of *Against the Odds* I reported that, as the apprentice jockey develops in experience, the performance of his charges and the return produced by backing them improves. I attributed this pattern in part to the apprentice's trainer, who will pair the rider with more able horses as his competence increases. I repeated this analysis with a larger sample and found the trend to be somewhat softer. The performance of three- and five-pound claimers is comparable to that of their fully-fledged counterparts whether one examines all runners or limits the sample to the top-rated. As expected, seven-pound claimers have a slightly poorer record than those receiving three- and five-pound claims. Notably, I feel my results give tentative support to the contention that the strength of apprentice and conditional riding is improving.

Leighton Aspell

CHAPTER 14

The Going

Of all the specific conditions associated with a race, the going is the most salient. On turf, moisture and rain soften the ground providing less resistance to the horses' hooves and reducing traction. Soft ground curtails a horse's ability to accelerate and reach its maximum speed. Accordingly, the amount of effort that is required to cover a given distance will increase. In National Hunt racing, the lack of resistance provided by soft ground impairs a horse's jumping ability but provides a better cushion on landing. The sheer weight and speed of a jumping horse coupled with the effects of gravity conspire to create very large compression forces on the frail equine fore legs. In fact, ground that is dry and hard can render jump racing dangerous during the summer months.

Rain and moisture tend to compact and harden the artificial surfaces. The various synthetic topsoils (i.e., Fibresand and Polytrack) respond to moisture and wear in different ways. For example, Fibresand (currently laid at Southwell) wears more easily than Polytrack (Lingfield and Wolverhampton). In November 2001, Lingfield replaced their Equitrack surface with Polytrack, a wax-coated synthetic riding surface that regains its original shape extremely well after hoof penetration. A similar move took place at Wolverhampton in the autumn of 2004, when the existing Fibresand track was replaced with Polytrack. Although Southwell has retained a Fibresand surface, it was re-laid in 2004 to provide a better consistency across all parts of the track.

I remember from my own experience that human sprinters always prefer a hard surface. However, a proportion of horses demonstrate a preference for soft ground due to various factors relating to their galloping action and physiology. It is not that some horses run faster on soft ground, just that they are less impeded than others. To return to the analogy with track and field athletics, I encountered several distance runners who were outclassed by a certain competitor on a synthetic track but closed the gap considerably when running cross-country because they coped well with the specific strength and postural demands of natural surfaces. Horses have a far more complex gait that humans, hence there is a greater potential for horses to demonstrate distinct preferences in terms of the racing surface. Indeed, Phil Bull felt that the going preferences of a horse should be the most important consideration when making a selection.

It is often remarked that extremes of going affect the likelihood that a race will be run according to established form. For example, when the ground is heavy,

Phil Bull

emphasis is placed on the ability of the runners to cope with the conditions underfoot and this effect randomises the results of races. Conversely, it has been suggested that when the ground is firm and running fast, favourites and horses with the best form will triumph on the flat. As stated above, the picture is rather different where jumping is concerned. For example, J. P. McManus advised backers to be careful when the going is fast during the Cheltenham Festival; he maintained that soft going was preferable for betting purposes. Please accept my apologies for returning to the subject of weight. However, another premise that one often encounters is that horses bearing the heaviest weights fare much worse when the going is soft. There is an intuitive logic behind all of these assumptions but that is not the same as hard evidence.

On the flat, favourites win more often on firm ground than on softer going. The strike rate on ground softer than good was 27.2%, a figure that increased to 31.3% when the ground was firmer than good. The best way to exploit this tendency is to lay favourites when the going is heavy. During the period of my sample, I found 136 odds-on favourites running on heavy ground. If you had laid each of these selections to lose £100 then the profit would have been £2,448; better than a poke in the eye with a jockey's whip. If favourites priced at under 2/1 are considered instead of merely those starting at odds-on, then the number of possible selections increases fourfold in exchange for a drop in profits from 18p (per £ staked) to 11p. In National Hunt racing, favourites also made poor betting propositions when the ground was riding heavy but no obvious opportunity for profit was forthcoming. A notable limitation of this analysis is that the going preferences of a horse are incorporated into the price on offer. For example, horses that are known to prefer soft ground are more likely to be made favourite when they encounter the right conditions.

One way to eliminate the effects of the market is to assess the performances of top-rated horses running on different categories of going. In National Hunt racing, the going exerted no consistent effect on the performances of top-rated horses. However, top-rated runners on the flat were subject to very much the same trend that was observed for favourites; both the strike-rate and profit level increased as the ground became firmer. For example, when the going was firmer than good, top-rated runners returned a strike rate of nearly 40% and a profit of 25p (per £ staked).

The total return to £100 stakes on each of the 251 runners was a princely £6,125. On heavy ground, the strike rate fell to 24.3% and backing every selection resulted in an 8p variable stakes loss.

In the case of top-weighted handicap runners, there was no consistent relationship between going, performance, and profit in National Hunt racing. Nevertheless, in keeping with conventional wisdom, top-weights running on heavy or soft ground provided fantastic opportunities for laying. When starting at odds beneath the 2/1 mark, laying these selections returned a profit of almost 22 pence per pound staked. This profit equates to £7,136 if each of the 328 runners had been laid to lose £100. I turned my attention to runners bearing the lighter weights (defined as those within 5 lbs of the 'bottom-weight' in each race). As predicted, these selections performed better and returned smaller losses when the ground was softer. For example, my National Hunt sample contained as many as 5,300 lighter-weighted handicappers that ran on soft or heavy ground. A slight loss (4p per £ staked) was returned by backing each of them, which is quite a statistic when one considers the dross that can often be found amongst the lower-weighted runners. In races run on good-to-firm or firm ground, the lower-weighted runners return a much higher 32 pence loss.

In flat racing on turf, the effects of weight also differ depending on the going. Top-weights perform poorly in heavy ground (SR = 7.8%, loss = 45p per £ staked) when compared to ground that is firmer than good (SR = 12.0%, loss = 18p). The opposite is true of horses bearing low weights (within 5 lbs of 'bottom-weight' in each race). On going that is soft or heavy, such runners return a profit of approximately 7p (per £ staked) if variable stakes are used. When the ground is running firmer than good, a large variable stakes loss of 30 pence is suffered by those backing horses with a light burden. Unfortunately, there are too few short-priced candidates to justify a laying approach.

GOING PREFERENCES

The going preferences of a horse are very difficult to identify statistically. However, I decided to make an attempt. I searched for flat horses that had run at least twice on going that was softer than good and at least twice on ground that was good-to-firm or firmer. I then calculated the horse's average speed rating on softer ground and on firmer ground. Those possessing an average rating that was at least ten lbs higher in softer conditions I termed 'soft' horses, and those displaying the opposite credentials I referred to as 'firm' horses.

TABLE 15. GOING PREFERENCE (GOING = GOOD TO SOFT OR SOFTER)				
GOING PREFERENCE	N	SR%	P	VSP
Soft horses	224	13.4	£0.50	£0.52
Firm horses	886	6.0	-£0.30	-£0.30

Table 15 demonstrates the importance of considering a horse's going preferences when the going is soft. Considering the simplicity of the approach, the level of profit derived is highly impressive. In fact, a £100 stake on each of the soft-horses racing on going that was softer than good would have netted you £11,200; a sum akin to a modest income annual (but without any income tax). If one broadens the sample to include all horses whose rating was at least five lbs superior in softer conditions then the number of qualifiers increases threefold yet the profits all but disappear. Nevertheless, if considerations other than the going were brought to bear on the selection process and bets were struck at exchange odds or on-course, then backing 'soft' horses on soft going could prove to be a lucrative strategy. I assessed whether or not 'firm' horses would perform better than 'soft' horses on going that was firmer that good. Although there was an improvement in strike rate in the expected direction (7.2% compared to 3.8%), this approach yielded no real advantage in terms of profit. Of the two tendencies, preference for softer ground is the more pronounced specialism. Hence, it is far more important to consider the going preferences of runners on the flat when the going is softer than good.

There are other methods of determining which type of going a horse prefers. For example, the number of placed finishes a horse has achieved on a certain type of ground is a strong indicator of how he will perform when those conditions are encountered again. A specific approach is to lay all fancied runners that have never achieved a placed finish on the prevailing going. I considered all flat races on ground that was softer than good and found 496 odds-on favourites that had never been placed on softer going after at least one attempt. To have laid each of these selections to lose £100 would have led to a profit of £5,456. Despite fewer qualifiers (n = 104), the approach worked equally well when applied to horses racing on firmer ground (firmer than good), which had yet to run into a place under similar conditions. A profit can also be generated by backing horses on soft ground that have demonstrated consistent ability to handle the surface. I sought runners that had achieved six or more places on ground that was softer than good. I found 238 qualifiers and, although the level of profit was impressive (32p per £ staked), the strike rate of just 10.9% was somewhat disappointing.

One word of caution: not all horses demonstrate marked going preferences. For example, an analysis I conducted led me to conclude that, when considering a bet on softer ground, it makes no difference whether a horse has performed well on firm ground previously (and vice versa). It is much more important to ascertain that a horse has failed to produce its expected form under today's conditions. this principle is demonstrated each March at Cheltenham when Irish raiders routinely triumph on good ground that they never previously encountered. The going preference variable (i.e., whether horses were 'soft' or 'firm') also influenced the results of National Hunt races. However, the effects were more subtle and the profits harder to find. For example, when running on softer ground, 'soft horses' produced a strike rate of 16.5% and a profit level of 13.5p (per £ staked). Contrast these figures with the performance of 'firm' horses who won only 9.5% of their races on softer ground (softer than good) and returned a loss of 42 pence. Notably, the consideration of going preference is complicated in National Hunt racing by the fact that the season is cleaved into two distinct periods: summer jump racing on firmer ground and the conventional winter programme which is normally contested on boggier surfaces.

In practice, one needs to be more interpretative than statistics allow for when assessing the going preference of a horse. If you review a chaser's form and discover that the horse won a hurdle race three years ago on the same heavy going that it will encounter again today, it is easy to jump to the conclusion (excuse the pun) that the prevailing conditions are highly suitable. However, the hurdle race may have been a poor contest against two other runners thus rendering the form irrelevant. In some cases, one will have to balance the form a horse has shown against its going preferences. Take for example a day on which the racecourse that you have chosen to attend resembles the Somme in 1916 (without the heavy artillery and trenches). If one should read the word 'mudlark' next to the name of a runner then an assumption that often follows is that the horse in question is a good betting proposition. However, there may be others in the race that do not revel in the conditions to the same extent, but whose form on heavy ground is better due to superior ability.

GOING REPORTS AND THE TRUE GOING

The real issue facing backers when considering the state of the ground is the sheer equivocality of going reports. Indeed, it could be said that the seven discrete categories of going belie the subtle variety of conditions under hoof. Until recently, the problem was that going was assessed in a fundamentally subjective way. The estimates were totally dependent on the clerk of each course, who naturally had a vested interest to attract runners and spectators. One of the worst ways to do this is to report ground that differs markedly from good.

In France, an instrument known as a 'penetrometre' has long been used to quantify the resistance provided by the turf. On these shores, attempts to develop an alternative to the penetrometre based around an instrument concealed in a man's shoe appeared to be quietly dying. However, a British equivalent to the Gallic device with the phallic name is finally being adopted. In fact, the imaginatively titled *Going-Stick* is considerably superior to the penetrometre in that it measures not only the resistance provided by the turf but also the degree of 'shear'; a term that refers to the amount of force required to pull the stick down to a 45° angle (with the ground) from an upright position. This objective system of going assessment has been extensively tested during 2003 and 2004 and, at the time of writing, the going stick is being used at 24 of the 59 British racecourses. The device produces a numerical reading that varies between 1.0 (heavy) and 15.0 (hard); a figure that can then be easily translated into the conventional going categories that we know and love.

When I go racing, I generally take the opportunity of walking the course and assessing the ground for myself. Conditions underfoot often vary dramatically from one part of the course to the other and even from one side of the track to the other, a subject that I will return to when discussing the effects of the draw. It is not uncommon for a morning of steady rain to alter the going from that which has been declared. Any change in the state of the ground can best be gauged by watching the action of the horses, especially when they approach the final furlong and fatigue begins to set in. In addition, observe the depth of the imprint that the hooves make in the turf. Another pointer is when the first race or two on the card goes to unexpected winners with better form on soft ground. One of the reasons I enjoy betting at Cheltenham is that the racecourse provides a radio service that enables me to hear interviews with the trainers in the parade ring via a small earpiece. Valuable information regarding the true going can be gleaned from the comments of trainers and jockeys.

Arguably, the most relevant method of assessing the state of the ground is to examine race times. Notably, going that has been officially described as 'good' has produced times that vary quite dramatically. It is especially illuminating to investigate finishing times after the first day of a festival meeting and conclude

Soft ground

that the going is slower or faster than advertised. Going is a mysterious concept, as the poor performance of a horse that has much winning form under the prevailing conditions can still be excused by its trainer because it "didn't like the ground". Indeed, the frequency with which unexpectedly poor runs are explained in terms of the horse's aversion to the ground borders on the suspicious.

Like love, going changes everything- even the length of a race. In very soft conditions, the additional time taken to run a race places an increased emphasis on stamina. Hence, if a horse can barely endure a mile and a half on good ground it almost certainly won't make it home when the rains come. When the ground is heavy, the distances that separate the finishers can become strung out to the extent that the runners are in different postcodes. Hence, the value of form achieved on heavy ground has no currency with that achieved on genuinely good racing ground. It's like comparing US dollars to Polish Zlotys.

CHAPTER 15

The Racecourse

In track and field athletics, each race under marathon distance is run on a course that is reasonably similar, regardless of the venue. If the sport of kings were configured in the same way then a horse's form would transfer very easily from one racecourse to another. However, the huge variation in the characteristics of the 59 British racecourses provides an edge for the intelligent backer. The significant features that distinguish each course are listed below:

- **Direction of turns:** Left-handed, right-handed, or a combination of both.
- **Undulation:** Ranging from the pancake flatness of Kempton Park to the alpine topography of Epsom or Goodwood.
- **Inclination of finish:** An uphill finish such as that of Cheltenham can prove to be a particular test of stamina.
- **Tightness of turns:** Ranging from the centrifugal circuit at Chester to the roman straightness of Newmarket's Rowley mile.
- **Length of finishing straight:** A less significant factor that can nevertheless affect the shape and outcome of a race.
- **Width of track:** Whereas Newbury's track is as wide as a country mile, the finishing straights at Goodwood and Pontefract are particularly narrow.
- **Size, construction, spacing, and designation of the fences:** The different designations of fence include water jumps, plain fences, and open ditches. However, this is a topic that requires a chapter of its own (see Chapter 20).

Kempton Park, a prime example of flatness in a course

The gradient at Cheltenham

The course at Chester demonstrates tight turns

The Roman straightness of Newmarket's Rowley Mile

Some of the above characteristics are determined by the length of the race. For example, the minimum trip of 5f is straight at most courses whereas any distance over 1m 2f will include at least one turn. I would offer a table that lists the characteristics of each course individually, but this information has been wheeled out in every racing book I have ever bought. Having seen thirty or so such charts containing broadly similar information I do not have the heart to bring another one into the world. In any case, it is very important that you develop a graphic knowledge of each course's distinguishing features based on your own experience of visiting them.

The consequence of such diversity across racecourses is that one must assess the extent to which the form from one course will transfer to another. The variable effectiveness of the thoroughbred at different venues is a highly significant factor. Indeed, this aspect of betting methodology has drifted into the vernacular ("horses for courses"). A classic example is provided every year when racing 'personalities' debate the likelihood that the winner of the 2000 guineas on Newmarket's wide, flat, Rowley Mile course will handle Epsom's tight, roller-coaster Derby course. Horses are highly sensitive to their environment and success at a certain type of course is a product of the animal's preference as well as the configuration of its physique. Fortunately, the neat categories that are used to describe the features of racecourses render this a subject that is highly suitable for statistical analysis.

One approach is to isolate a variable such as the direction of turn, and identify horses that are suited to either left-handed or right-handed tracks. This analysis proved to be a most daunting analytical task and I attempted many variations before producing a technique that allowed me to mine some respectable profit. In the first edition of *Against the Odds*, I compared the ability ratings of flat horses when running at either left- or right-handed tracks. This scenario is reminiscent of the task I faced in identifying 'soft' and 'firm' horses in the previous chapter. Hence, I used a broadly similar method to compile a list of 'left' horses and 'right' horses; i.e., animals that had performed better at left- and right- handed tracks respectively. When I limited the sample to courses with tight bends, I found that 'right' horses yielded higher returns than 'left' horses when racing on right-handed courses. Unexpectedly, an equivalent result did not materialise when I analysed the performance of 'left' and 'right' horses running on left-handed tracks. The only reason that I could proffer to explain this result was that left-handed tracks outnumber right-handed tracks on the flat by a ratio of nearly two to one. Hence, preference for right-handed tracks may constitute something of a specialism.

In the present edition, I shifted my focus to National Hunt racing; a domain in which the direction preference (i.e., left or right) of a horse is thought to have a greater influence on its performance than on the flat. Despite serial fine-tuning, I could find no difference in the performance of 'left' and 'right' horses so I sought an alternative method of designating the direction in which each horse preferred to race.

After several unsuccessful attempts that were focussed on the number of wins that had been achieved when racing in different directions, I hit upon a more promising tactic that revolved around placed performances. For the purposes of this test, 'placed' referred to a finish in the top three. I identified horses that had placed at least three times previously when racing in the same direction as the race I was analysing, yet had never achieved a place when running in the opposite direction. For example, I looked for runners at Cheltenham that had placed at least three times at left-handed courses such as Aintree but not at right-handed courses such as Sandown. On right-handed courses, the 466 selections won 25.5% of their races and returned a profit of 24 pence per pound staked. If betting with the customary £100 stake then a profit of some £11,184 would have resulted. On left-handed courses, the trend was not as clear. Indeed, it was only when one considered horses that had been placed at least seven times on left-handed tracks that profits began to materialise. In conclusion, the direction preference of a horse is not a factor that is easy to establish statistically. There may be individual examples of horses that exhibit a marked preference for racing either right- or left-handed but my research indicates that they are in a minority.

Another course characteristic that influences the outcome of races is the curvature of the track. I investigated the performance of horses that had achieved at least two more placed finishes on straight tracks (e.g., Newmarket) than on curved tracks (e.g., Chester) in races under 9 furlongs in length. When racing at straight tracks, top-rated runners that had already demonstrated a preference for straight tracks returned a profit of 18p (per £ staked). On the contrary, backing top-rated horses that had achieved at least two more places on curved tracks than on straight tracks led to a loss of 26p. To a lesser extent, I found an equivalent result when I examined the performance of top-rated horses running at curved tracks. There does appear to be some scope for the layer as well as the backer in following this approach; 123 runners started at odds-on when racing in a straight line despite never having achieved a placing on a straight track. If one had laid them all to lose £100 then the return would have been a fetching £3,936 (32p per £ staked). When laying odds-on favourites it is very unusual to record a profit level as high as 32p because a large percentage of the selections will usually still win. Despite fewer qualifiers, the same approach yielded good results in reverse, i.e., when I attempted to lay favourites racing on curved tracks that had only been placed at straight tracks previously.

I could have continued analysing each feature of every racecourse in painstaking detail but instead I opted for a more comprehensive method. The various dimensions that define the nature of each racecourse must combine to render courses similar or different in a general sense. The path I followed was to assess the value of form from a given track when applied to the other tracks. In so doing, it was possible to plot the relationship of each track to the others in terms of form. The precise technique that I used was to locate instances when two consecutive runs occurred at different courses and compare the respective speed ratings. For example, 807 runners followed a race at Ascot with one at Newbury. The average improvement between these runs was four lbs per horse. Hence, we would expect a horse running at Newbury following an outing at Ascot to produce a performance four lbs in excess of its previous effort.

Slightly more maths was involved but I have relayed the basic gist of the analysis. My results were liable to be confounded by the way that horses are aimed and placed by their trainers. For example, runners are routinely entered into preparation races at small tracks that prepare them for the greater spoils offered by elite courses such as Epsom, Ascot, Newmarket, Cheltenham, and Aintree. Nevertheless, a reliable index of likely improvement is still of value to the backer, even if the differences in performance from one course to the next are influenced by factors other than the different characteristics of the two racecourses.

To develop the 'standard differences' in lbs between each pair of courses I used data from the flat seasons 1999-2002. If I had assessed the relationship between the 'expected improvement' and profit using the same dataset then my results would have been invalid. For example, having already proven that horses that raced at Kempton following a run at Ascot performed a lot better at the latter track then there would obviously be a strong likelihood that backing each of those runners at Kempton would have produced a profit. The real proof would stem from testing the 'expected improvement' standards with a new set of data (2003 & 2004). The results indicated a potential for profit. In my second dataset I found 106 runners that were expected to produce a performance that was six lbs superior to that of their previous run. The resultant profit from backing each of these runners was an impressive 53 pence per pound staked (£6,148 to £100 stakes). Although the sample is somewhat small, the result is encouraging when one considers that the only factor determining the selections was the two racecourses in question.

Having demonstrated the general principle, the next step was to investigate the patterns of profit that related to backing and laying runners at each individual racecourse. In order that the results were more robust, I considered the profit that was returned in each year over a period of five seasons leading up to 2004. I eliminated any combination of courses which did not yield at least three profitable seasons from the last five and two profitable seasons from the last three.

Any runners that started at odds of less than 2/1 were considered for laying purposes and the results are displayed in Table 16.

CODE	BET	HORSES RUNNING AT:	FOLLOWING A RUN AT:	N	SR%	P	VSP
Flat	Backing	Newcastle	Newmarket (July)	84	25.0	£0.43	£0.52
		Sandown	Newmarket (Rowley)	140	20.7	£0.52	£0.55
		Nottingham	Salisbury	115	18.2	£0.39	£0.89
		Pontefract	Sandown	67	23.9	£0.72	£1.06
		Pontefract	Lingfield (turf)	65	23.1	£0.27	£0.97
		Pontefract	Ascot	85	23.5	£0.40	£0.79
		Pontefract	Chepstow	59	18.6	£0.48	£0.93
		Bath	Ripon	53	22.6	£0.36	£1.26
		Bath	Ascot	69	23.2	£0.24	£0.73
	Laying	Wolverhampton (AW)	Southwell (AW)	157	64.3	£0.18	—
		Wolverhampton (AW)	Wolverhampton (AW)	245	60.4	£0.06	—
		Brighton	Brighton	34	61.8	£0.13	—
NH	Backing	Newbury	Cheltenham	196	19.4	£0.32	£0.56
		Uttoxeter	Chepstow	148	18.2	£0.55	£0.66
		Ludlow	Cheltenham	74	20.3	£0.35	£0.31
		Doncaster	Newbury	74	23.0	£0.66	£0.74
		Huntingdon	Ascot	60	25.0	£0.46	£1.11
		Newton Abbot	Southwell	89	19.1	£0.46	£0.52
		Perth	Wetherby	85	20.0	£0.45	£0.64
	Laying	Fontwell	Fontwell	46	71.7	£0.21	—
		Huntingdon	Huntingdon	30	56.7	£0.13	—

TABLE 16. PREVIOUS APPEARANCE BROKEN DOWN BY RACECOURSE

In absolute terms, the most profitable course combination to emerge from the analysis was backing horses at Uttoxeter following a run at Chepstow. If each of these runners had been backed with a £100 stake then a profit of £8,140 would have ensued. The results are all the more impressive for the constraint I placed that ensured a minimum of three profitable years during the five years of the sample. Yet it is a sobering thought that none of the combinations listed in Table 16 showed a profit in every year although horses running at Sandown following Newmarket came very close as did runners at Perth following Wetherby. Of course, it is likely that the results are not just due to the similarities between the racecourses but the timing of certain race fixtures and the manner in which trainers like to place their runners. However, it is notable that no single trainer sent out more than three winners from any of the combinations listed in the table.

There are a couple of general trends relating to the analysis that merit comment. Firstly, the majority of the laying bets are horses running consecutively at the same course. This pattern also applies to many other courses that do not appear in Table 16 because the respective profits were not consistent enough over time. This result does not mean that fancied horses re-appearing at the same venue run poorly. Instead, such selections appear to be too heavily supported by the general public. Indeed, if a horse has produced a strong recent performance at the same course then the chances are that every bastard and his dog will know about it.

The majority of the bets listed in Table 16 that involve backing a horse might be described as follows: A runner that has stepped down from a race at a prestigious course to a smaller, more provincial venue. Regardless of the actual value and class of the races concerned, contests held at the more elite venues (e.g., those associated with classic races) are generally more competitive. Such a simple observation might form the basis of a betting system in itself.

It is important to assess each transition from one course to another on its merits. An interesting example is provided by runners that make their way to Aintree via Cheltenham. Principally, this group is derived from horses that run at the Cheltenham Festival and then progress to April's Grand National meeting. For several reasons, this is a very difficult to double to achieve. Consequently, many short-priced favourites are beaten at Aintree when they fail to reproduce their Festival runnings. Depending on the calendar in that year, the two meetings are somewhat squashed together so as to prevent a full recovery after the saga of Cheltenham's championship races. Moreover, because of the Festival's prominence within the National Hunt season, most horses are trained to peak at Cheltenham.

Rough Quest

As I explain in Chapter 17, a peak must generally be followed by a slump before another zenith can be reached. As spring begins to take hold the ground is often a lot harder in early April at Aintree that it was three weeks earlier in Gloucestershire. Add to this the marked dissimilarity between the two courses and there are several reasons to be sceptical of short-priced runners at Aintree that are attempting to record a famous double. A better sign is a competitive placed run at Cheltenham that serves as a springboard for Aintree. For instance, Rough Quest produced a fine jumping performance in the 1996 Cheltenham Gold Cup prior to his exhilarating victory in the Grand National under Mick Fitzgerald.

As revealing as an all-encompassing statistical analysis can be, the suitability of a racecourse for each horse depends very much on the individual preferences of the animal. To understand these equine dispositions requires the opportunity to observe the horse in action so as to relate the animal's preferences to observations regarding its physique and galloping action. Nevertheless, the variety inherent in British racecourses provides an opportunity of showing a profit to backers of both the expert and systematic persuasions.

CHAPTER 16
The Time of Year

THE SHAPE OF THE RACING YEAR

One of the constraints the backer faces is that racing follows distinct seasonal patterns. Hence, if your specialist subject is two-year-olds then you are going to be very bored between November and May. The flat season begins with a flourish in late March at Doncaster and the character of the racing passes through several distinct shades until the curtain falls in late autumn. The first Saturday in November marks the traditional point at which the season returns to its beginnings at Doncaster and the cycle is complete. Due to the programme of summer jump racing, the National Hunt calendar spans the entire year. However, the diluted schedule of summer racing on faster ground is very much an interlude; there are no major races and the majority of horses are rested and prepared for a winter campaign. In the months between May and September, National Hunt racing sleeps with one eye open.

The first truly big meeting of the season is the Paddy Power Open at Cheltenham, which is normally held on the second weekend in November. From this point onwards there is a measured build up towards the crescendo of the championship races that fill a three-day festival in mid March at Cheltenham. Aintree's Grand National meeting in early April serves as a climax to the season and offers many races that are commensurate in value to their Cheltenham equivalents. The Betfred (formerly Whitbread) gold cup, contested at Sandown on the last weekend of April, is the final valuable race of the jumps season and marks its official end. Symbolically, the card at Sandown on that day is "mixed" and includes both flat and jumps races. After this equinox, the baton of our attention is passed on to the flat while jump racing trots off to the summer pastures of Stratford, Uttoxeter and Market Rasen.

The flat season on the turf is characterised by a string of celebrated meetings at courses such as Doncaster, Newmarket (Rowley Mile and July courses), Chester, York, Ascot, Goodwood, Epsom, Newbury, and Sandown. The shape of the season is rather skewed, as it reaches its Zenith in June with the Derby and Oaks at Epsom followed very quickly by the Royal Ascot fixture. The final classic meeting is held at Doncaster in mid-September to accommodate the St. Leger. From this point onwards, the season freewheels towards its indeterminate conclusion in early November. Hence, the contours of the jumps and flat seasons are most dissimilar: The measured, incremental build-up of the National Hunt calendar resolves into a finale equivalent to the cup final or championship game of a football season. Conversely, the flat season on the turf takes off like a rocket and burns up on re-entry. Under either code, the valuable televised races act like coat pegs from which the rest of the season is hung.

The Lincoln Handicap at Doncaster – the curtain-raiser on the Flat

Summer jumping at Newton Abbot

The Grand National

While all this is happening, the all-weather season continues like a steady beat in the background. The fixture list limps through the summer from April to October while it is eclipsed by its turf equivalent. The lion's share of the fixtures take place between November and March, during which time almost three-quarters of all-weather races are held.

SEASONAL TRENDS AND BETTING

I have often read that backers should avoid betting at the beginning and end of each season, as profit is less likely. I have also noticed a seasonal trend in my betting performance whereby I always flourish in May and June but appear to 'hit the wall' in July. Notable bettors such as Graham Wheldon have also reported that their otherwise profitable selections perform poorly at either end of the flat season. There are several reasons for these seasonal variations in betting performance. At the beginning of the season, fields are large and there is no recent form available. The form that is generated by these early races takes a few weeks to settle down as horses rapidly regain full racing fitness or improve on their debut performances while others re-emerge belatedly carrying good condition. Furthermore, the weather is more likely to be unsuitably cold and wet at the start of the season. As the summer months draw on, horses that have been heavily campaigned become jaded and those that have been well rested can re-emerge to overturn established form. At the season's end, weather conditions deteriorate once more and opportunities to race become ever sparser. Field sizes increase again as trainers enter their charges for races while they still can.

In the following analyses I have attempted to ascertain seasonal variations in the performances of market favourites and top-rated horses in non-handicaps. The loss returned from backing market favourites on the flat at different times of the year is fairly constant at around seven pence per pound staked. The only exception is that favourites running in the first three weeks of the season return a relatively large loss approaching 13p. In fact, if one had laid each of the 310 odds-on favourites in my sample that ran in March and April then a profit of £3,160 would have resulted.

In all-weather racing, favourites do very poorly at the start and end of the main season (months of November and March). Interestingly, if you had backed favourites on artificial surfaces during the summer months of June to September then you would have broken even thus indicating that the form in question is most reliable. In National Hunt racing, there are no worthwhile trends save for an interesting blip in March when favourites do poorly; a result that may be attributable to the Cheltenham Festival. Indeed, starting on the first day of the Festival in 1962, 22 consecutive favourites went down!

In National Hunt racing, the performance of top-rated horses in non-handicap races is somewhat erratic throughout the year and no clear trend suggests itself. On the flat, top-rated horses perform poorly at both ends of the season as depicted in Graph 7. It is clear from the graph that SR% and profit are closely related as one would expect. Interestingly, the performance of top-rated runners appears to peak twice, once in June and then again in September. This trend seems to confirm my own anecdotal observations of a mid-summer slump. In a wider sense, the graph conveys the effectiveness of conventional form analysis throughout the year. At certain points in the season, form appears to be somewhat equivocal thus rendering betting conditions less favourable. Viewed from a different angle, the unreliability of both mid-summer and early-season form may present an opportunity for the shrewd bettor who opposes the crowd. Much like market favourites, top-rated runners on artificial surfaces perform well in the summer months.

What do all these trends mean? It is clear that backing horses on the flat in March and early April is a very haphazard occupation; the laying option may prove more advantageous. The smaller fields, firm ground, and settled form that coincide in the early summer months may favour you if typically select fancied runners. However, if like myself you select horses with longer prices about them then these conditions could impinge upon your profit. For example, when betting in maiden races, I always make my best profits of the year between late April and Royal Ascot in June.

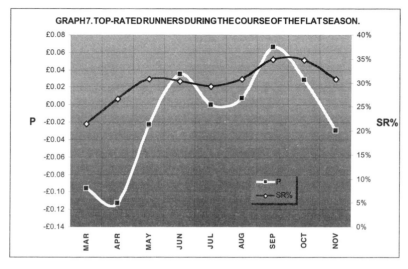

GRAPH 7. TOP-RATED RUNNERS DURING THE COURSE OF THE FLAT SEASON.

From this point onwards, the racing gods seem to lose favour with me and I have to look at other types of races for betting opportunities. The best advice I can give you is to keep records (not in your head!) and examine them to discover the seasonal trends that may apply to you. If I were more honest I might paraphrase Mark Twain and suggest that March and April are two of the peculiarly dangerous months to bet on horses, the others being September, February, July, January, December, August, May, November, June, and October.

Royal Ascot

Fitness CHAPTER 17

THE PHYSIOLOGY OF FITNESS

In order to appreciate the importance of fitness, it is beneficial to have a grounding in the subject. Almost without exception, information in betting books regarding the exercise physiology of horses is ludicrously inaccurate. What follows is based on literature that accompanies the equine science certificate, a course that is taught at the University of Limerick.

The term fitness covers different types of physical conditioning that the animal develops through an appropriate combination of racing, training, nutrition, and rest. The development of cardio-vascular fitness underpins all strenuous equine activity. *Cardio-vascular fitness* refers to the ability of a horse's heart and vascular system to transport oxygen from the lungs via the bloodstream to the working muscle cells where it is used to provide energy from foodstuffs. This energy is then used for the muscular contractions and extensions that are necessary to propel the horse. Such a means of deriving energy is referred to as aerobic metabolism (with oxygen). As a species, horses are especially good at transporting oxygen, indeed the maximum rate of oxygen uptake in a horse is some 3-4 greater than that of a healthy, fit human male. Training can increase the maximum oxygen uptake of a horse by up to 20 per cent, after which a plateau is reached.

Aerobic metabolism can support a steady state of exercise below a certain threshold (e.g., trotting or standing) for a considerable period of time. When working above this threshold, the horse requires an additional source of energy that is derived chemically in the muscle cell by a process known as *anaerobic metabolism* (without oxygen). Hence, when performing relatively intense activities such as galloping and jumping, the horse must also draw on anaerobic energy pathways.

Although anaerobic metabolism can support intense activity, the process relies upon chemical substrates that are in limited supply. Furthermore, anaerobic metabolism leads to the production of *lactic acid,* which accumulates in the horse's muscle cells and impedes contraction. The effects of lactic acid can be observed in the closing stages of races, especially long National Hunt races in which the runners are brought to a standstill. The *lactate threshold* represents the point at which lactic acid begins to accumulate because it is being produced faster than it can be removed. In terms of fatigue, the lactic threshold is the beginning of the end. Oxygen is required to clear or *buffer* excess lactic acid, which is the principal reason that you are out of breath after bounding up the stairs or performing some similar burst of strenuous activity. In thoroughbreds, the ability to tolerate lactic acid is especially responsive to training. It is worth bearing in mind that, in relative terms, horses have far better cardio-vascular systems than humans. Even in sprints, around 80% of the energy a horse utilises will be generated aerobically. This is why respiratory fitness is such an important characteristic of a racehorse. Indeed, when being interviewed after a race, a horse's jockey and trainer can often be heard to pay considerable attention to the animal's breathing patterns.

Lochsong: the classic five furlong sprinter of recent times

The development of cardio-vascular and respiratory fitness lay the foundations for more demanding work that promotes developments in the equine musculo-skeletal system such as increased muscle size, contractile power, co-ordination, and flexibility. The essential principle that underlies such conditioning is one of adaptation. A stress is imposed on the horse and an adaptation occurs so that the physical structure concerned can more readily cope with that stressor in the future. For example, a five-furlong sprinter will tear muscle fibres during every race and these will be repaired during the horse's recovery. The muscle in question will be marginally stronger when it is next called upon to contract in a race. When the source of stress is removed, the adaptations become redundant and are reversed in order that the body can be more efficient; unnecessary muscle tissue merely wastes energy. All such adaptations will reach a natural, genetically determined plateau.

Horses working anaerobically

It is important to realise that even at the end of its three-year-old season, a horse is not fully mature. The rapid process of equine maturation leads to sharp increases in stamina. For example, seven furlongs represents an endurance event for two-year-olds; juveniles that demonstrate the stamina to endure that distance will subsequently develop into middle-distance horses. Skills such as breaking from the starting stalls or clearing an obstacle in jump racing require a very specific type of fitness which must be carefully schooled under the supervision of the trainer. Following rehabilitation from injury, a footballer might develop a high level of cardio-vascular or muscular conditioning, yet due to his lack of recent playing experience he is said to not be 'match fit'. The same principle applies to horses; general conditioning is no substitute for specific skills that require co-ordinated patterns of muscular contraction.

If the intensity, frequency, or duration of the races and training sessions is too high then the horse will be over-trained, its performance will suffer, and its whole immune system will be compromised. Like human marathon runners who undergo intensive training regimens, racehorses are especially vulnerable to viral infection. Thoroughbreds are genetically predisposed towards athleticism because of the manner in which they are bred. However, the price of this superior ability is fragility. Think of cars: I can drive my family runabout over a bump in the road with impunity but if I tried to do the same with a formula one racing car I would mutilate its computer-assisted suspension system.

The propulsive features of the horse are exaggerated in the thoroughbred; the long thin legs, powerful gluteal musculature, and elongated tendons predispose the animal to injury. In addition to these concerns, the attitude of the horse to training and racing must be managed. The coaches of human athletes experience considerable difficulty motivating their charges to commit themselves to punitive regimens of physical training. However, trainers of horses are faced with the additional obstacle of having to motivate animals. The psychological trauma of strenuous work can sour the commitment of a horse and induce a treacherous and perverse attitude. Hence, for a variety of reasons, it is understandable that trainers err on the side of caution when developing the fitness of horses in their keep.

INDIVIDUAL FITNESS PROFILES

Each horse possesses a unique tolerance to training: some will thrive on regular work whereas others are of a more delicate persuasion. The latter type requires briefer, less-intense training sessions that are interspersed with long periods of recuperation. Like human athletes, horses are trained in cycles as fitness is built up to a peak that can only be maintained for a relatively short period of time. Living organisms are not machines and the body must be periodically relieved of stress in order to continue developing. If one could plot on a graph the performance ratings achieved by a horse in each of its races, the result would not resemble a straight line but a wave containing multiple peaks and depressions. Graph 8 is a lifelong performance profile of the popular Irish chaser *Moscow Flyer*. I have taken the liberty of identifying the gelding's failures to complete using distinctive black marker points. At one stage in his illustrious career to date, Moscow Flyer was famous for falling or unseating his rider on every fourth outing while winning all the others. If all horses conformed to such neat patterns then I would be living on my own Island off the coast of Fiji, and yours would be the next one down.

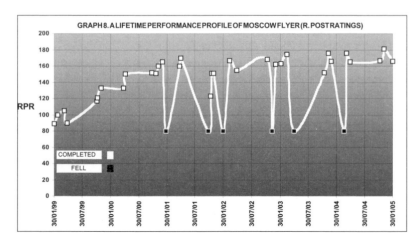

On many occasions, poor runs can be explained by unsuitable conditions. However, even if the racing conditions were unchanging, the performance level of a horse would probably not be constant over time. This concept is vital to understand because most bettors look at a series of performances and assume that an improving trend will continue or that a horse will produce a run that is equivalent to its previous effort. Each horse may have its own performance curve as unique as a signature and the skill is to anticipate the shape of it based on what you know about the fitness of the horse. This is much like predicting when a share on the stock market has bottomed out or reached its ceiling. Such judgements are much more possible when you have had the opportunity to see the horse in the flesh at different points during the season and assess its physique and the manner of its performances.

When set within the context of such individual differences, it seems like folly to assess the fitness of a horse using an approach that can be applied to every runner. However, just as all horses are different, they are all somewhat alike and general patterns can be of utility to the bettor. I decided to investigate the performances of horses according to the interval between successive runs. In flat racing (turf) horses that reappear quickly offer the best potential for profit, especially in handicap races. Indeed, handicappers returning to the racecourse after less than four days return a small profit of three pence (per £ staked). This may be because such runners have re-appeared before they are penalised for a victory by having their handicap mark raised. The frequency of races that handicappers can notch up means that race fitness is an especially important factor in these contests. In fact, laying odds-on selections that have not raced for at least three weeks is a good option. Although I was only able to locate 74 such runners, the return was a fantastic 33 pence per pound staked; a very high profit level for laying odds-on horses.

Considering the *exposure* that a horse has had to racing over the last 100 days can also lead to profits on the flat. Underexposed handicap runners are good candidates for laying. I found 118 odds-on favourites that had enjoyed less than three outings in the past 100 days. If one had laid each of these to lose the customary £100 then a considerable profit of £2,827 would have appeared on your Betfair balance statement (24p per £ staked). For all but the elite, a low frequency of races is somewhat unusual in handicap circles, possibly indicating some injury or lack of soundness on the horse's part. In non-handicaps, it also pays to lay fancied horses that have not raced for a long time. I found 211 runners that had been absent from the course for at least 200 days yet started at a price below evens. If one had laid each of these selections to lose £100 then the resultant profit would have been £3,804.

Curiously, overexposure is a positive factor in flat non-handicap races. I found 408 runners that had raced at least ten times in the previous 100 days. If a variable stake had been used to minimise the investment in hopeless causes then a return of 21p (per £ staked) would have been shown. However, it is possible that this sample included several performances by the same horses. The importance of fitness becomes especially clear when we examine the performances of top-rated horses in non-handicap races; a group that produces a high strike-rate by default. As expected, backing runners that returned after less than four days led to a high level of profit. Although I only found 94 such selections, 30 of these won returning a profit of £2,632 to £100 stakes. Of even greater interest is the strong performance of top-rated runners that had benefited from a break of between three weeks and one month; apparently an optimal period of recuperation. A strike rate of 37.9% was complemented by a profit level of 22 pence per pound staked (£8,184 to £100 stakes). Selections returning after 31-60 days also performed well (SR = 32.7%, profit = £0.10).

It is often said that juvenile horses require more rest than their mature counterparts. In the first edition of Against the Odds I was able to report, as expected, that two-year-old runners that returned to the racecourse after less than two weeks performed very poorly. However, when I repeated the analysis over a longer timeframe of five years I found that the pattern of results was very erratic year on year. Surprisingly, in 2003 and 2004 juveniles that raced after a interval of less than eight days performed respectably. Maybe this changing trend reflects the greater precocity that is being shown by two-year-old horses in recent times. Several commentators have asserted that racehorses are being bred and trained to win at an increasingly younger age so that they can quickly return some of their owner's investment. Nevertheless, it was still possible to profit from laying fancied juveniles that raced within a week of their previous contest. There was also a profit to be made by opposing two-year-old runners that had never seen a racecourse before. I found 352 such runners that started at prices under 2/1 and if you had laid them all to lose £100 then the profit would have been £5,280.

Each year, the punting masses seem mesmerised by the latest crop of glamorous juveniles. Without even proving that they can canter in public, these undoubtedly fine-looking specimens are backed down to ridiculously short prices by those who are convinced that they are about to witness the debut victory of Dubai Millennium's heir. If backing an odds-on favourite is ill-advised then supporting one that has never stepped onto a racecourse is daft. This sort of behaviour allows bookmakers and other professional gamblers to go enjoy exotic holidays and drive sports cars.

In National Hunt races, broadly similar trends are found although to a lesser degree. In handicaps, the best strike rate was shown by runners returning to the racecourse after a week or less. However, this factor is clearly taken into account in the prices on offer and there is little advantage to the backer. There is an angle for the layer in terms of opposing all runners that have not raced in 200 days or more. I discovered 240 such selections priced at under 2/1 and the return per pound staked was an encouraging 15 pence. In non-handicap races, I found no clear opportunities to develop profits. Runners returning after a break of between four to seven days ran well as did those that benefited from between three weeks and one month's rest. When I focused on top-rated animals I found that a modest profit ensued from backing those runners returning within a week (14p per £ staked). Interestingly, despite a relatively low strike rate of 33.9%, top-rated competitors that were sidelined for 200 days or more produced a respectable profit (13p per £ staked) thus indicating that these runners were under-supported by the general betting public. The conventional wisdom must be that a horse cannot win without a recent run despite having displayed good form in relation to the other runners in the field.

There is an orthodox view that the fitness requirements of a race depend on the distance run. For example, performance in longer races is thought to benefit from a lengthy recovery whereas it is commonly held that sprinters can notch up a series of runs in a short space of time. I was unable to find any concrete evidence of this contention in flat or jump racing. My own tentative opinion is that the alternative possibility may be true: Although longer races require more energy, shorter contests are more likely to lead to strain and injury due to their higher intensity.

FITNESS: A CONCLUSION.

Clearly, 'fitness' is a multi-dimensional concept and it is necessary to ask *what sort of fitness?* Considering the fitness of a horse has never led me directly to many winners. However, I have been able to avoid a host of losers and this is of equal importance to my overall profitability. Where possible, I consider fitness on a horse-by-horse basis rather than trying to apply general rules. Paying close attention to the physical appearance of horses when on course helps me immeasurably in this regard. Finally, the key consideration when appraising the fitness of a horse is the trainer. Acquaint yourself with the handler's record in developing and maintaining racing fitness in her charges.

The Draw CHAPTER 18

THE SIGNIFICANCE OF THE DRAW

The drawn allocation of starting stalls is a vital factor to consider when contemplating a bet on the outcome of a flat race. Although the draw doesn't impact upon every race, in many contests the inherent bias can make the difference between winning and losing. Even in races where no draw bias is expected, the previous form of the runners may well have been shaped by the influence of the draw on other courses.

The draw

The subject is a constant source of interest among successful bettors because, by its very nature, the bias is always shifting and creating opportunities to gain an edge in the fight for profits. Research into the effect of racing from different starting stalls first rose to prominence in the United States where it became a veritable science long before the topic was popularised in Britain and Ireland. The contemporary preoccupation with the draw in this country was ignited by the work of several eminent backers, in particular Graham Wheldon, who became synonymous with the subject after writing a series of books. The premise of backing favourably drawn horses is disarmingly simple but therein lies the problem. Raw data reveal trends that are often ambiguous and require very careful interpretation. In most cases, other related factors such as the going and the field size need to be taken into account.

Racing publications are infested with superficial treatments of the draw's effects which have become meaningless and token: "Back high drawn horses at Beverley but not at Chester." Ironically, the awareness that the betting public has gained of the more prominent draw biases has rendered them profitless. Simplistic rules belie the subtlety and complexity of the draw's effects. Indeed, copious books have been written on the subject of the draw alone. Hence, there is only space here to outline the principles at work.

The position of a horse in the starting stalls provides us with an important clue as to how the runner concerned will be incorporated into the contest. A race is a sequence of connected events and the initial place that a horse assumes in the field will predetermine its opportunities to succeed in the latter stages. Energy expended in order to gain a position at the start of the race can exert a disproportionate effect on fatigue levels in the closing stages. Furthermore, energy wasted due to encumbrance in running can predispose a horse to rapid fatigue when an effort is required towards the business end of the race. Any unnecessary acceleration or deceleration is highly inefficient and will bring the horse closer to its lactate threshold (see previous chapter). Hence, the importance of the draw affects the running of the race as a whole.

The factors that determine the effects of the draw bias:

1) Curvature of the track. In track and field athletics, a staggered start is used in 200 and 400m races. Those athletes starting in the outside lanes receive an advantage to compensate for the additional distance that they must run. In horse races, acquiring the coveted position on the inside rail around turns often depends on the draw. The centrifugal effects are greatest on the horses running on the outside flank of the field because those on their inside will push them even wider. Even if there is a considerable run-in prior to the first turn, horses drawn in the outermost stalls must expend a lot of energy to cut across the field and negotiate a position close to the inside running rail. The alternative is to miss the break and adopt a position at the rear of the field that may be highly disadvantageous in the latter stages of the race. The acuity (tightness) of the turns varies depending on the course and the distance of the race. This is one reason why the draw bias should be considered separately for each race distance run at a given course. For example, races over 7f at Ayr and 1m at Bath start from a chute that joins the main course like a tributary stream after 100 yards or so.

2) Proximity to the running rail. The running rail serves as a reference point and helps horses to run in a straight line. On very wide courses such as the Rowley Mile at Newmarket, the field may bisect into two groups, one adhering to each rail.

When horses remain in a single group that occupies the centre of the course, those that are 'covered up' in the heart of the field often gain an advantage over horses which are more exposed at the periphery of the group.

3) The going. The condition of the ground is seldom identical across the width of the track. When the going is soft, the strip along the inside rail may become muddier and more distressed after each race. This effect becomes progressively worse throughout the season. If the ground close to the inside rail becomes very sticky then the typical draw bias is often reversed because those runners on the outside of the field benefit from running on faster ground. The artificial surface Fibresand (Southwell) wears fairly easily and this has the effect of creating a slower strip of ground adjacent to the inside running-rail after successive races. The camber of the track (slope from one side to the other) and the drainage of the soil or artificial surface will affect the prevalence of slower patches of ground. The type of watering used on the course will also exert a marked effect on the condition of the ground. For example, the seasoned race-reader Alan Amies noted that the effects of the draw at Thirsk depend on whether the track has been watered or natural rainfall has occurred. This observation is probably also true of sprints at Catterick.

4) The size of the field. The draw bias is partly determined by the size of the field. In a two-runner race, the horses concerned will be racing over practically the same ground whereas in a field of 25 runners, two horses drawn at opposite ends of the starting stalls will effectively be running in different races. The conventional wisdom is that the draw bias is exaggerated by large fields and simply does not exist in small fields; propositions that I will test shortly.

5) The distance of the race. It is often contended that the draw exerts a greater influence over shorter distances (under 1m) because there is less opportunity to recover from a weak start.

6) The racing preferences of the horse. Some horses are more likely than others to exploit a good draw and dispute the early lead whereas others produce their best performances when they are covered up and brought slowly into a race. A favourable draw would be wasted on a horse that prefers to race with the pack rather than at the head of affairs.

7) Jockeyship. An advantageous draw provides a jockey with an excellent hand, but he still has to play his cards right. On many occasions an incisive piece of riding can completely equalise the effect of the draw. An enterprising rider may have the opportunity to seize the initiative and locate faster ground. The best example of this phenomenon that I can recall was Darryl Holland's ride on *Knavesmire Omen* in the 2m½f handicap at Doncaster on the final day of the flat season in 2002. The heavy ground had created a quagmire along the normal racing line, which Holland avoided by bringing the Mark Johnston-trained gelding across the track onto the faster ground adjacent to the far rail. Although

Knavesmire Omen had covered far more ground when he rejoined the pack around three furlongs from home, he was able to contest the lead. Crucially, he had conserved energy during his detour and he was able to maintain his gallop as the remainder of the field fell away leaden and spent.

KNAVESMIRE OMEN wins at Doncaster, November 2002

8) The position of the stalls on the track. At some racecourses, the starting stalls are occasionally moved to occupy different positions across the width of the track. Such alterations can completely reverse the effects of the draw. There are also times when a running rail will be moved in order to unveil a strip of fresh ground. Unfortunately, not all such modifications are properly reported or recorded thus presenting a headache for most bettors but an opportunity for those organised enough to undertake detailed research and contact the racecourses in person.

The army of different factors listed above serves to create much confusion and pave the way for all sorts of quackery and fiction. It is inadvisable to provide prescriptive rules concerning the effects of the draw at a particular course due to the inherent variability of the bias. Those who make the attempt soon become lost in a forest of contradictions and caveats:

Yarmouth (LH): In short sprints (under 7f) one should favour runners drawn low but only in small fields. In larger fields, the bias is completely reversed and those drawn high enjoy the best of it except in handicaps where there is no real trend. If it rains, then horses drawn in stalls three and four hold the upper hand except if the stalls are placed on the far rail, in which case the high-drawn runners prevail. If the ground is hard then all of the aforementioned biases are exaggerated, with the exception of the bias relating to large fields, which is reversed (but only in maiden races). Check to the see if the racecourse has been using their tractor to assist with watering and drainage. If this is the case then there will be a strip in the middle of the course that will run faster and horses drawn in stalls six and higher (races under 9f) will hold all the aces (except stall nine, which has been cursed by local travellers). When a strong wind is coming in from off the sea then horses running on the far rail have a terrible record (except over 1m 2f when the wind will ruffle their manes and inspire them towards excellence). Keep a close eye on the caravan site near the 1m 6f start because the presence of holidaymakers unnerves the horses and some miss the break (but only in June). None of the above applies on Tuesdays or during the World Bowls Championships.

The difficulty lies in the fact that the draw bias is organic; it seems to be constantly developing and changing. Hence, a bias that holds during one meeting may not apply to the next one. Furthermore, a racecourse that was felt to have a strong draw bias for several years may take steps to eliminate it; partly because the presence of a very apparent imbalance angers trainers, who are in the position of carefully preparing horses for races which are not fair contests. The work that racecourses undertake appears to have mixed results: Whereas Haydock succeeded in almost reversing their established bias, Chepstow have made attempts that appear to have accrued only a temporary neutralisation. Statistical techniques are apt to flounder in the face of a fluid phenomenon such as the draw. However, there are appropriate methods of analysing the draw statistically; either by taking a very broad view or an extremely narrow one.

THE DRAW BIAS AND THE CURVATURE OF THE TRACK

I have long contended that the curvature of the track is the most important of all the factors to consider when attempting to predict the effects of the draw. I feel that a bias is almost always present in races that involve curved sections of track. I analysed the results of all races that were run around bends and evaluated the performance of the two innermost stalls, i.e., those stalls closest to the inside rail. Thus, if the race in question featured a left-handed turn then the innermost stalls would be numbers one and two.

Races with turns in both directions (e.g., the figure of eight at Windsor) were eliminated from the analysis. I compared the performance of the two innermost stalls, the two outermost stalls, and the remainder of the field (i.e., excepting the two innermost and outermost stalls). I reasoned that despite its crudity, this approach would provide an effective mapping of the draw bias under the various conditions that I chose to select. Generally, if one examines the performance of runners that start from a particular stall (e.g., stall 4) then the results have little meaning. Whereas stall number one is always situated on the 'inside' of the track (when turns are left-handed), stall number eight may be in the middle of the field or on the wide outside depending on the number of runners. I chose the two innermost stalls in order to increase the sample size while still isolating the effects of an inner draw. The results for all races that qualified are displayed in Table 17:

Going round the bend

TABLE 17. THE DRAW IN RACES RUN AROUND A TURN				
STALLS	N	SR%	P	VSP
Innermost two	17,970	11.6%	-£0.19	-£0.07
Middle	68,611	8.1%	-£0.30	-£0.16
Outermost two	18,081	9.8%	-£0.32	-£0.16

Although the effect is not enormous by any measure, the findings demonstrate the importance of backing horses that have the shortest distance to cover in a race. Indeed, to have produced a variable stakes profit in a sample of nearly 18,000 runners would require divine intervention. Notably, horses drawn on the outside marginally outperformed those runners in the centre of the field. Hence, the draw bias in this case is not a smooth effect that impedes runners more and more the further they start from the inside rail. Research I have undertaken in the past has shown that those drawn in the middle of a field are generally at a disadvantage. Nevertheless, the best opportunity to earn a profit came from laying odds-on runners that were unfortunate enough to be drawn in the outermost two stalls. I found 341 runners who met these criteria, if one had laid each to lose £100 then a profit of £6,479 would have been earned. The profit level of 19p per pound staked more than doubled to 42p when only races of eight runners or more were considered, although the number of qualifiers dropped to 84.

Does the draw bias remain the same regardless of the size of the field? Firstly, I had to eradicate the skewing effect of the field size on strike-rate percentages: If all horses were created equal then a typical runner in a two-horse race would have a 50% strike rate, whereas in a 20-horse race the figure would drop to 5% purely by virtue of the larger field. Once this distortion was corrected it emerged that the draw bias became more extreme as the field size increased. Races with between five and nineteen runners seemed to be similarly affected by the draw. It was only in very large fields of twenty or more runners that the influence of the draw had a stronger bearing on the result. For example, I found that backing all handicap runners drawn in the innermost two stalls when the field size was 20 or more yielded a very acceptable profit of 23p (per £ staked). If each of these selections had been backed to the tune of £100 then a profit of some £12,164 would have graced your bank account with its presence. In the above example I restricted the sample to handicap races. Nevertheless, in most other cases, handicaps do not provide a better environment to exploit the effects of the draw bias as is so often assumed. From a logical perspective, why should a strong draw bias just disappear because a given race is not a handicap?

I found that the race distance did not significantly alter the draw bias. Although unexpected, this finding was not entirely surprising; both the 2m 2f Cesarewitch handicap and the 1m 6f Ebor handicap are highly dependent on the draw. The going conditions may sometimes entirely reverse the known draw bias as they do in sprints at Catterick. Nevertheless, I found that the bias favouring runners with an inside line was just as prominent on soft or firm ground. On all-weather surfaces, I struggled to pinpoint the effect of the draw at all. Indeed, the bias that existed on turf appeared to have been inverted: Runners drawn in the outermost stalls performed the best and incurred the least heavy losses when backed. In fact, it was hard to escape the conclusion that runners adjacent to the inside rail made very good laying fodder. The only possible explanation for this unexpected finding might have been that those drawn in the innermost stalls were impeded by an uneven strip of ground that had been distressed by the hooves of runners in previous races on the card. Indeed, almost all of the races in my sample took place before the 2004 resurfacing work was undertaken at Southwell and Wolverhampton. In particular, the new Polytrack surface at Wolverhampton is specially designed to regain its shape well after hoof penetration.

I used aerial photographs and maps of the racecourses to calculate the degree of turn that was encountered during the course of each race. For example, in 1m 2f 75y races at Chester, the runners complete a circuit of the course and the degree of turn is therefore 360°. Although the overall degree of turn had little effect on the draw bias, the tightness of the turns did. For example, whereas the runners navigate a full circuit and several turns during 1m 2f 75y races at Chester, an arc of only 90° is encountered over a similar distance at Brighton. The draw bias was much greater in races with tighter turns than in those with shallower turns. In races with a degree of turn that was at least 270° per mile, I pinpointed 145 market favourites that were fortunate enough to occupy one of the two innermost stalls. If you had placed £100 on each of these selections you would have achieved a profit of £6,660. Despite the small sample size of 145, the level of profit (46p per £ staked) is high enough to encourage the conclusion that these returns are not the result of blind chance. Furthermore, a strike rate of over 50% is always welcome.

PROFITABLE STALLS

A far more specific technique that I favour is the identification of 'profitable stalls'. Quite simply, if you were to back every runner drawn in a profitable stall, then you would win money. In order to simplify this task, I focussed on the horses that were drawn in the two lowest and highest stalls in each race. So as to ensure that these stalls are likely to produce a profit in the future I applied three criteria: Firstly, a profitable stall must have sent out at least fifteen runners in each of the entire seasons that were included in my sample. Secondly, the stall should have produced a variable stakes profit in at least four of the sample's five years. I included stalls that had only seen three years profit under the proviso that both 2003 and 2004 were profitable years. Lastly, I verified that the stall had produced both an overall profit and a variable stakes profit over the period of the sample. The results are displayed in Table 18.

TABLE 18. ANALYSIS OF PROFITABLE STARTING STALLS								
COURSE	DISTANCE	STALL	CONDITIONS	N	SR%	P	VSP	ANNUAL PROFITS
Bath	5f 11y	H1	Any	114	15.8	£0.02	£0.61	01111
Beverley	7f 99y	H2	Any	146	14.4	£0.05	£0.49	10111
Beverley	7f 99y	H2	Softer than good	132	15.2	£0.12	£0.54	11111
Brighton	6f 209y	2	Any	132	15.2	£0.38	£0.65	10011

TABLE 18 CONTINUED								
Brighton	6f 209y	2	10 or more runners	80	15.0	£0.62	£0.71	10111
Brighton	6f 209y	H2	10 or more runners	85	11.8	£0.31	£0.35	10111
Brighton	6f 209y	H2	Good or firmer	100	17.0	£0.30	£0.48	10111
Brighton	6f 209y	2	Handicaps	72	13.9	£0.03	£0.35	10111
Brighton	11f 198y	2	Good or firmer	65	23.1	£0.16	£1.03	11010
Doncaster	6f	H1	Any	119	10.9	£0.05	£0.29	01011
Doncaster	7f	H2	Any	120	14.2	£0.99	£0.78	10011
Doncaster	7f	H2	10 or more runners	97	13.4	£1.34	£0.82	10011
Epsom	7f	1	Softer than good	75	24.0	£0.42	£0.92	10011
Goodwood	7f	H2	Good or firmer	91	19.8	£0.08	£0.66	01111
Goodwood	7f	H1	Good or firmer	86	19.8	£0.24	£0.68	01011
Hamilton	6f 4y	H1	10 or more runners	65	12.3	£0.40	£0.43	01011
Hamilton	6f 4y	H2	Softer than good	113	15.9	£0.04	£0.28	11111
Hamilton	6f 4y	H1	Softer than good	107	15.0	£0.19	£0.32	01011
Hamilton	9f 35y	H2	Any	91	15.4	£0.42	£0.33	10011
Haydock	7f 31y	2	Softer than good	68	13.2	£0.10	£0.18	10011
Leicester	5f 218y	1	10 or more runners	65	15.4	£0.60	£1.05	11011
Leicester	5f 218y	1	Any	150	16.0	£0.48	£0.75	11011
Lingfield (Turf)	7f	H2	10 or more runners	120	10.0	£0.04	£0.15	01011
Lingfield (Polytrack)	8f	2	10 or more runners	185	14.1	£0.33	£0.53	X1011
Newcastle	5f	2	Softer than good	77	18.2	£0.91	£0.63	10111
Newmarket (Rowley)	7f	2	10 or more runners	103	12.6	£0.31	£0.57	10111
Newmarket (Rowley)	7f	2	15 or more runners	65	12.3	£0.31	£1.03	10101
Newmarket (Rowley)	8f	2	Any	126	15.1	£0.18	£0.71	10011
Newmarket (July)	7f	H2	10 or more runners	90	10.0	£0.05	£0.18	10111
Newmarket (July)	7f	H1	10 or more runners	86	12.8	£0.09	£0.68	00111
Newmarket (July)	10f	H2	Softer than good	73	19.2	£0.25	£0.71	10111
Pontefract	10f	1	10 or more runners	65	10.8	£0.32	£0.29	11011
Redcar	6f	2	10 or more runners	69	11.6	£0.33	£0.59	00111
Redcar	6f	2	Softer than good	89	12.4	£0.20	£0.42	00111
Ripon	10f	H1	Softer than good	74	25.7	£0.20	£1.06	10011
Salisbury	6f 211y	H1	Softer than good	101	11.9	£0.35	£0.40	00111
Sandown	7f 15y	2	Any	81	21.0	£0.19	£0.86	11011
Windsor	6f	H2	Handicaps	68	13.2	£0.33	£0.27	01011
Wolverhampton	5f	H2	10 or more runners	130	13.8	£0.04	£0.56	10011
Wolverhampton	16f 44y	H2	Any	80	12.5	£0.47	£0.16	10111
Yarmouth	8f 2y	2	Softer than good	75	13.3	£0.09	£0.59	00111
Stall: H1 = Highest drawn. H2 = 2nd Highest drawn.								
Annual Profits: 11111 = every year in profit, 00001 = only final year in profit etc.								

The fluidity of the draw is very much in evidence: I only found two stalls that produced a profit every year (at Beverley & Hamilton) from the 1,524 that I tested. Far more common was a blistering profit one season followed by a sharp loss the next. No wonder the draw bias is such an oft-debated subject in the racing media; it changes like the weather so there are always new angles to discuss. Another salient point is that one must be very specific when highlighting a profitable stall.

Simply because stall two at Brighton (6f 209y) is highly profitable to follow, this does not necessarily mean that the same stall will produce a profit when the race distance is a furlong longer (7f 213y). According to Table 18, very few racecourses boast profitable stalls at different race distances. Certainly, when the two innermost or outermost stalls are both seen to be in profit then an especially strong trend has been identified. For example, in the case of 7f races at Goodwood both the highest and second highest draws led to consistent profits. The impressive conclusion is that nearly 40% of races over 7f at Goodwood were won by horses that were drawn in the highest two stalls. What poor value must the other runners have represented? This idea simply had to be tested. I found 84 favourites starting at less than 2/1 yet not drawn in the two higher stalls. To have laid each of these to lose £100 would have resulted in a profit of £2,016.

Of special interest is the fact that many of the well-known biases such as that existing at Chester are not represented in the table. Presumably, this absence is because the prices on offer have been reduced to deny a consistent edge to backers. Furthermore, the analysis highlights profitable draws that are largely overlooked by the betting public and racing media. When did you last read about the strong, year-on-year bias over 7f at Newmarket's Rowley mile course? Another aspect of the findings is that runners drawn in the stalls on the extreme flanks of the field (1 and H1) fare worse than those drawn next to them (stalls 2& H2). In fact, stalls 2 and H2 outnumber stalls 1 and H1 by 29 to 12 in my analysis of profitable stalls.

It may be that an extreme draw is too isolated or that both the outermost and innermost runners are liable to being squeezed against the rail. So which is the most profitable stall in the land? The clear winner appears to be the second-highest-drawn stall at Doncaster in races over 7f. If one had simply backed each runner from this starting stall with a £100 stake then £11,800 would have been earned. Apologies for infusing this impressive statistic with a sprinkling of reality; however, the profit in 2000 would have been nearly £11,000 followed by a loss of £4,300 the following year and a further £1,000 loss in 2002. The final two years of the sample would have each seen profits of over £3000. Even when the profit over a five-year period is so high, there is still a sense of Russian roulette in following this particular approach. In a nutshell, that's the whole problem with betting on horses; it's not a steady wage.

INTERPRETING THE DRAW BIAS

Although the scope of my analyses was limited, I hope that I have highlighted the importance of the draw and the impotence of betting methods that fail to account for it. How do you incorporate the effects of the draw into your betting decisions? A formbook might tell us that low-drawn runners often prevail at Chester. But what it is a low draw? Anyone would tell you that stall number one is low, but what about stall four in a ten-horse race? Do you still bet or do you elect to keep your powder dry? This problem is exacerbated by the convention of trisecting the stall numbers into low-, middle-, and high-drawn runners. Such a technique leaves us with the following scenario: the advice of the formbook or racing paper is to back low-drawn horses in a particular race that has nine runners. Therefore, if our selection is drawn in stall three, we conclude that the horse has a favourable draw and we make the bet. However, if the hypothetical steed starts from neighbouring stall number four, we consider the horse to be drawn in the 'middle' and refrain from betting.

The draw bias simply does not operate in convenient geometric patterns. We cannot say that as the stall numbers increase, so the advantage held by each successive runner will diminish in an incremental fashion. As we have seen, when a bias exists that favours low-drawn horses, it is quite normal for those runners drawn on the opposite flank to fare better than those drawn in the middle of the field. The runners that are housed in stalls one and two may have a fantastic record, whereas those situated in stalls three and four may fare very poorly because they are often impeded by the horses drawn immediately inside them. This factor was borne out to some extent by my analysis of profitable stalls. What is needed from a bettor's point of view is a method of quantifying the draw bias stall by stall; preferably presented in a graphical form for ease of comprehension. This is a searching task that I have not attempted to address here for one good reason: Peter May has already developed an excellent method in his recent book *Horseracing. A Guide to Profitable Betting* (Raceform, 2004; see page 46).

I suspect that the best approach is to develop expertise by reviewing recordings of previous races. Naturally, if you visit the same course regularly then the solution presents itself, as you are able to keep a diary of sorts as you go. Using this technique, it may be possible to form an opinion about the shape of the races and what part the draw played in forming this pattern. In such cases, judicious reasoning and the experience of watching races will beat abstract statistical analyses every time. It is not always possible to make a profit simply by backing well-drawn runners and laying those that are assigned poor starting berths.

A more sophisticated modus operandi is to locate runners whose form is over-rated because they were flattered by a good draw on a previous outing. Runners that have been impeded by a poor draw and yet have still run creditably are of even greater interest. In such instances, there is a genuine possibility that the betting public might collectively underestimate the relevant form and allow a runner to start at an inflated price. Always be prepared to revise your opinions about the draw bias at a particular track as it is liable to change very swiftly. The essential drawback with using statistics in racing and betting is exaggerated when we consider the draw: By the time I have been able to identify a profitable trend, the underlying bias is likely to already have collapsed! The advantage of this variability is the possibility of staying one step ahead of the market and finding opportunities to bet at favourable odds. I have found the relationship between the draw bias and the market to be haphazard and although a few of the more obvious biases are incorporated into the prices that are on offer, most are not.

It is worth relating that my current interest in the draw stems from an experiment that I undertook four years ago. I reviewed my betting records relating to the previous summer and classified all my bets as well drawn, moderately drawn, or poorly drawn according to indications provided in the formbook that I used at the time. I found that my well-drawn selections yielded far more profit than my moderately drawn selections; however the 'poorly' drawn selections yielded the most profit of all! This test has made me sceptical of the standard interpretations of the draw bias that I encounter in the racing press. By the way, please accept my apologies for the bland and functional chapter titles in this book. Other betting writers seem to have formed a guild and resolved to bejewel their book chapters and articles with titles that contain quietly hilarious puns. With this in mind, I had wanted to call the chapter you're reading "quickest on the draw" until I realised that I would have to come up with such masterpieces for every other chapter as well. Never mind, at least you have been spared "going, going, gone" and "courses for horses".

Class CHAPTER 19

THE DIFFERING LEVELS OF COMPETITION

When evaluating the performance of a horse, it is essential to consider the strength of opposition that it faced. The different strata of races described in Chapter 4 provide a framework whereby horses can compete with runners of similar ability. The resultant hierarchy resembles the different divisions of the football league; I would not back the winner of a Class 5 regional race to beat the winner of the Epsom Derby for the same reason that I would not back a non-league football team to beat the Premiership champions. Both teams may excel in their given stratum of competition, but the Premiership team would have more 'class', a word which simply denotes a higher level of ability. In order to illustrate the difference in performance between horses competing in races of different classes, I present a comparison of winning times. This idea is not new; I based the following tables on those produced by Nick Mordin over a decade ago in his seminal book *Betting for a Living*. The race times that I used were corrected for the relevant going allowances and the standard times that applied to each course and distance. Because of the timeframe of the sample, my analysis is based on the old classification structure of flat racing that was replaced in 2004 (see Chapter 4).

On the flat, the fastest times were recorded by the horses that had won the most valuable races (first place prize money over £100k). Hence, I have used the times clocked in such races as a reference point. The figures in Table 19 express how many seconds longer it took the winners of other races to complete a furlong when compared to those running in the most valuable contests. The figures that denote the different types of handicap races refer to the official scale as it stood prior to reclassification in September 2004; e.g., a 0-70 handicap is only open to horses with an official rating of 70 or lower.

Table 19 provides us with an approximate understanding of the different levels of competition in flat racing. If you want to imagine the time differences in terms of lengths, then ten hundredths of a second would equate to around six lengths. Hence, a Group 1 winner would be expected to beat a Group 2 winner by around three lengths. First-place prize money actually provides a better indication of the level of competition than the official grade of the race. Logically, faster horses are entered for the larger prizes. It is worth noting that this relationship is determined by the prize money brackets that I have chosen and is not really linear as it first appears.

TABLE 19. TIME DIFFERENCES [SECONDS SLOWER PER FURLONG] BETWEEN THE WINNERS OF FLAT RACES

ALL RACES		1st PRIZE (£):		HANDICAPS	
Class A (Group1)	0.00	100k +	0.00	Listed	0.12
Class A (Group2)	0.04	50k – 100k	0.07	0-110	0.12
Class A (Group3)	0.06	30k – 50k	0.08	0-105	0.13
Class A (Listed)	0.12	20k – 30k	0.11	0-100	0.16
Class B	0.20	15k – 20k	0.13	0-95	0.19
Class C	0.19	10k – 15k	0.18	0-90	0.21
Class D	0.30	7k – 10k	0.21	0-85	0.24
Class E	0.30	5k – 7k	0.25	0-80	0.26
Class F	0.35	3k – 5k	0.30	0-75	0.30
Class G	0.39	Under 3k	0.35	0-70	0.30
Class G	0.40			0-65	0.33
				0-60	0.35
Selling races	0.26			0-55	0.34
Maiden races	0.26			Selling	0.26
Amateur Jockey	0.25			Apprentice	0.26
Apprentice Jockey	0.26				

NB: Time differences (seconds slower per furlong) in comparison with winners of valuable races (first prize > £100k).

For example, the difference between a £2,000 race and a £32,000 race is relatively large whereas little separates a £170,000 race from a £200,000 race. The winning times relating to handicap races provide some justification for the revision of the handicap divisions. While there is a clear difference in performance between the highest and lowest grades of handicap, there appears to be too many bands. Furthermore, several of the bands are insufficiently distinct from each other. Table 19 did not include races with age restrictions (e.g., 2yo races); these are presented separately in Table 20.

TABLE 20. TIME DIFFERENCES BETWEEN WINNERS OF AGE-RESTRICTED FLAT RACES

	1st PRIZE £5k-£10k		1st PRIZE £10k-£30k		1st PRIZE > £30k	
MONTH	2yo	3yo	2yo	3yo	2yo	3yo
APRIL	0.44	0.29		0.20		
MAY	0.43	0.27	0.31	0.20		0.12
JUNE	0.47	0.29	0.34	0.22	0.27	0.09
JULY	0.42	0.28	0.30	0.20	0.19	0.10
AUGUST	0.40	0.29	0.34	0.21	0.24	0.14
SEPTEMBER	0.39	0.30	0.29	0.15	0.17	
OCTOBER	0.38	0.25	0.26	0.19	0.15	

NB: Time differences (seconds slower per furlong) in comparison with winners of valuable races (first prize > £100k)

The results may appear somewhat haphazard because they represent a conglomeration of five seasons' times that should ideally be assessed on a horse by horse basis rather than simply averaged. Nevertheless, it is still possible to discern the improvement in speed that results from the maturation of horses during their first two years of racing. The development that occurs during the winter break between the ages of two and three is quite evident, as is an uneven improvement during the course of the season itself. Notably, the times recorded by two-year-olds in September and October are notably faster than those recorded in April and March. Tables 21 and 22 reflect the different levels of competition in all-weather and National Hunt racing respectively.

TABLE 21. TIME DIFFERENCES BETWEEN WINNERS OF ALL-WEATHER RACES

NON-HANDICAPS		HANDICAPS	
Class A	0.02	0-105	0.00
Class B	0.00	0-100	0.02
Class C	0.05	0-95	0.06
Class D	0.20	0-90	0.06
Class E	0.19	0-85	0.10
Class F	0.21	0-80	0.23
Class G	0.28	0-75	0.16
Class H	0.32	0-70	0.19
Selling races	0.23	0-65	0.24
Amateur Jock.	0.24	0-60	0.24
Apprentice Jock.	0.23	0-55	0.24
Maidens	0.23	Selling	0.18
		Amateur Jock.	0.19
		Apprentice Jock.	0.17

NB: Time differences (seconds slower per furlong) in comparison with winners of 0-105 handicaps

TABLE 22. TIME DIFFERENCES BETWEEN WINNERS OF National Hunt RACES

NON-HANDICAPS		HANDICAPS		1st PRIZE (£):	
Class A	0.03	Graded	0.07	Over £100k	0.08
Class B	0.29	0-150	0.07	£50k – £100k	0.00
Class C	0.28	0-145	0.09	£20k – £50k	0.01
Class D	0.36	0-140	0.10	£10k – 20k	0.15
Class E	0.41	0-135	0.16	£5k – £10k	0.28
Class F	0.40	0-130	0.16	£3.5k – £5k	0.36
Class G	0.45	0-125	0.27	£2k – £3.5k	0.39
Class H (>£3.5k)	0.51	0-120	0.25	Under £2k	0.47
Class H (<£3.5k)	0.48	0-115	0.30	NOVICE RACES	
ALL RACES		0-110	0.32	Over £20k	0.00
Selling	0.34	0-105	0.39	£10 – 20k	0.15
Amateur Jockey	0.34	0-100	0.38	£5 – 10k	0.28
Conditional Jockey	0.34	0-95	0.42	£3.5 – 5k	0.35
		0-90	0.44	£2 – 3.5k	0.39
				Under £2k	0.48

NB: Time differences (seconds slower per furlong) in comparison with winners of races with a 1st prize of £30–100k

In the National Hunt sphere, the fastest times were not actually recorded by the horses contesting the best prizes. The winning times from races with first prizes of over £100k were actually slower that the times from the prize-money bracket beneath. This result is hard to credit although maybe it is due to the fact that the highest bracket contains many of the idiosyncratic races that jump racing is most identified with such as the Grand National itself. It is worth noting that, unlike in flat racing, the majority of National Hunt's greater prizes are handicap races; the principal exceptions being the Cheltenham championship races (e.g., The Gold Cup). Interestingly, the results show that the best novices produce amongst the fastest times. This finding supports the contention that the cream of the younger horses may be on par with their older rivals in terms of fitness.

In Table 22 I have combined the winning times relating to chases and hurdle races as I found little difference between the two disciplines. Notably, there is a difference in class between valuable hunter chases (Class H) and their more earthly counterparts. The same is true of National Hunt flat races that are excluded from the analysis because the absence of obstacles renders any comparison meaningless. In both National Hunt and all-weather racing, the handicap scale proved less accurate than in flat racing on turf. In particular, the steps between the different grades on the scale appear somewhat uneven. For example, there appears to be scant difference between the all-weather handicap bands with upper limits of between 55 and 65.

MOVING UP OR DOWN IN CLASS

My analysis of race times showed that prize money proved to be a more reliable indicator of the standard of a race than its official class. Accordingly, the BHB's decision to ally its new flat racing structure to prize money brackets appears to be the correct one. Many betting approaches are built upon the concept of following horses that are migrating up or down in class. The seasoned perspective is that horses which are descending in class are the more favourable betting proposition because they merely have to reproduce the level of ability they have already shown in order to be competitive; runners that are going up in class must improve. Furthermore, a horse that finished down the field in a valuable event may have been tailed off by its jockey when its chance had gone. If such a horse were entered into weaker event in which it could compete, one might expect the animal to produce a faster run. I set out to examine these propositions by assessing the effects of increases and decreases in class.

I divided the races into the same prize-money bands that I used in the series of tables above (Tables 19-22). For each prize-money band (e.g., under £5,000), I assessed the performances of horses that had previously raced in each of the other brackets. In general terms, it is preferable to follow those horses that are being dropped in class as they perform much better in terms of strike rate than those runners that are raised to a higher level of competition. Nevertheless, this difference in performance is factored into the prices that are on offer.

Horses are lowered in class for a variety of reasons. Whereas some horses are raised or dropped in class to enable them to win races, others are promoted optimistically by their owners or lowered because they have been hopelessly outclassed. I was able to exclude this 'noise' from the data by concentrating on top-rated horses. In contrast to expectations, profits resulted from backing top-rated flat horses that were raised in class as opposed to those that were lowered. In particular, horses that were raised in class by 50 to 100% (i.e., entered into a race worth between one and a half and two times more than the previous start) produced an excellent profit of 37p per pound staked. If one had backed each of the 449 selections that fulfilled this criterion with £100 stakes then a profit of £16,387 would have been earned. Notably, the 1,429 top-rated runners that were lowered in class by a similar degree won as many races (SR = 39.5%) but produced a loss of 7p per pound staked. In the highest echelon of flat racing, experience is clearly essential. For example, whereas group one favourites that had ascended from listed company were profitable to lay, those which had made the opposite journey were profitable to back.

PERFORMANCE OF FAVOURITES AND TOP-RATED RUNNERS IN DIFFERENT CLASSES

I examined the performance of favourites competing in different grades on the flat and found that market leaders had a poor record in Class A events. In fact, odds-on favourites actually proved profitable to lay (11p profit per £ staked). The reason for this finding may be that high publicity surrounds the runners in prestigious races; certain horses become widely tipped and consequently heavily bet on by the general public thus creating false favourites. I also took the liberty of ascertaining how top-rated runners performed in races of different value. In flat and national-hunt racing, top-rated runners returned the best profits when competing at the highest level (Class A).

On the flat, top-rated horses running in races with a first prize of over £50,000 performed with particular distinction. A profit of 17.5p per pound staked was complemented by a strike rate of 32.6%. If the usual stake of £100 had been placed on each selection then a profit of £4,463 would have been generated. In fact, simply backing top-rated horses with a rating over 110 on the flat (Raceform rating) led to an acceptable level of profit. I found 735 such runners in flat non-handicaps; 252 of them won (34.3% SR) and the profit to £100 stakes was an encouraging £11,760.

I was able to find an even better theatre of operations by focusing on younger horses. In National Hunt racing, top-rated runners aged six or less won an impressive 40% of races in Class A, returning a handsome 26p profit (per £ staked). A stake of £100 placed on each of the 188 selections led to a profit of £4,888. In top handicaps, it may also pay to follow highly-rated runners. For instance, topweights running in the very best flat handicaps (Class A) returned a fantastic profit of 78p per pound staked. However, the very high level of profit must be weighed against the fact that only 68 qualifiers were found.

THE NEW CLASSIFICATION SCHEME FOR FLAT RACING

By highlighting the lack of clarity evident in the previous framework, the results presented in this chapter provide evidence to support the introduction of the revised classification scheme. Prior to the modifications, the quality of a race was far more closely associated with the level of prize-money on offer than the nominal class or grade of the contest. The streamlined divisions and tighter structure will make the sport more appealing to lay-people who should find racing easier to follow. Because change is involved, not everyone connected with the industry is turning cartwheels across the floor. However, I consider the move to be a forward-thinking one that will benefit the sport not least because it shows that its governing body is willing to embrace change. New betting opportunities will almost certainly be created and naturally this is an excellent prospect.

Of course, analysts like me will encounter technical problems when we use datasets that span both classification systems. However, this disadvantage is more than outweighed by the fact that the new system will provide a better framework for research owing to its clearer structure. At the time of writing, the new scheme is still putting down roots and consequently any trends are yet to reveal themselves. At present, the configuration of National Hunt racing remains unaltered. However, should the amendments prove successful it is highly probable that National Hunt will only be one jump behind in assimilating the changes into its code.

Jumping CHAPTER 20

My career in hurdling lasted about four minutes; that was time enough to convince my athletics coach that hurdles and me went together like Superman and Kryptonite. Nevertheless, I have spent a long time watching humans and horses clearing hurdles and other obstacles. In both cases, the superior jumpers invariably beat the fastest runners. The example I gave of Amberleigh House in Chapter 6 demonstrated perfectly the extent to which the skill of jumping can eclipse speed.

From a physiological perspective, the ability to cover distances of two miles or more at speed and the ability to jump require completely different types of strength that may not necessarily coexist. Indeed, the genetic profiles of the best jumpers are similar to those of sprinters on the flat. Horses that lack explosive strength expend greater energy when jumping and very quickly reach the fatigue levels that I discussed in Chapter 17. The key concept to understand when considering the effect of jumping on performance is momentum. If you have ever watched athletics on television then you have probably heard David Coleman or Sally Gunnell elaborating on the importance of 'getting that trail leg down with a snap'. Some momentum will always be lost at the hurdle, but the best in the world become so by reducing this effect.

Gloria Victis

The real problem caused by a loss of momentum is that a runner is required to accelerate and thus waste energy. Think of a bad driver who accelerates rapidly between speed bumps and is forced to apply his breaks heavily; he uses far more fuel than a sedate driver but doesn't reach the end of the road much faster. To make matters worse, inexpert jumpers often check their stride and decelerate into obstacles, which exacerbates the energy costs of the whole endeavour.

Good jumpers must possess explosive strength, but above all they should be fluid and thus able to accommodate obstacles at speed. Jockeyship is of more importance in National Hunt racing than on the flat because the balance, strength, and skill of the rider can make a huge difference to the accuracy of his mount's jumping. It is important to recognise that steeplechase fences are not merely larger versions of hurdles. Whereas hurdles can be brushed through, fences must be cleared; the technique required is very different and much more demanding. Just as you should be wary of horses making their hurdling debuts, you should also be apprehensive of an animal that is stepping up from hurdles to fences. When the horse is thrown in, you won't know whether it will sink or swim.

The jumping ability of a horse is not a subject that lends itself to statistical analysis not least because the quality of jumping requires a subjective assessment. Nevertheless, I sought to investigate the returns that followed backing runners which fell on their previous appearance. There are various ways that a horse can fail to complete the course: the saddle can slip, the horse can refuse to jump, be brought down by another horse, stray from the marked course, be pulled-up by its jockey, be carried off the course by another horse, unseat the rider, or simply fall.

a jockey balancing a horse over a fence

The strike rate of hurdlers who completed the course on their last outing is twice that of those who failed to do so. However, this difference in performance is more than accounted for by the odds on offer. Nevertheless, it is worth laying hurdlers that fell or unseated their riders on their previous racecourse appearance. I found 132 such competitors that started at odds of less than 2/1; to have laid each of these to lose £100 would have resulted in a profit of £3,018. Hurdlers that had fallen in at least one of their previous three starts were also opposable. I found 236 runners which met this criterion and started at odds of less than 2/1. To have laid each of them to lose £100 would have produced a profit of £2,832. Falls in steeplechases do not exert a large influence on subsequent performance and what evidence there is suggests that this factor is accounted for in the prices on offer. This marked difference between hurdlers and chasers with poor jumping records might be explained by the fact that falls are more common over fences. Consequently, horses that fail to negotiate hurdles are more likely to be poor jumpers *per se*.

A noteworthy finding relates to horses that refused in one of their previous three starts. Chasers that refused to jump on either their second- or third-last run crept towards profit whereas the 163 hurdlers that fitted this description returned an uncanny profit of 71p per pound staked. If each of these had been backed with a £100 stake then a profit of £11,569 would have followed. Do such hurdlers represent a stock of rapidly improving animals or are they simply underbet by the crowd? In any case, it is clear that backing hurdlers that refused on their previous start is unprofitable (loss of 16p per £ staked). Such runners may require a further race and a completion in order to regain lost confidence.

We are often told that particular courses such as Ascot or Cheltenham have especially 'stiff' (rigid) fences that set a stern jumping challenge. Surely, form that is acquired at such tracks must be of greater value than that gained on courses with softer fences. For each racecourse, I calculated the total number of fallers, horses that refused, and horses that unseated their riders per 1000 fences faced. After an investigation, I concluded that confounding factors such as the going, the level of competition (e.g., Class A), and the size of the field did not influence my results greatly so I proceeded without accounting for them. I reasoned that the frequency of fallers at each course might change over time much like the draw bias so I produced figures for each season from 1999-2000 to 2003-2004. The 42 racecourses were then ranked in order of the frequency of fallers during each season and the results are displayed in Table 23 – see over the next page.

TABLE 23. NUMBER OF FALLERS PER FENCE FACED: RANKING OF National Hunt COURSES					
COURSE	1999-2000	2000-2001	2001-2002	2002-2003	2003-2004
AINTREE (NATIONAL) *	1	25	23	1	2
AINTREE (MILDMAY) *	16	5	2	2	3
ASCOT *	26	39	39	17	37
AYR	14	4	12	7	6
BANGOR-ON-DEE	30	34	33	24	17
CARLISLE	43	24	25	42	32
CARTMEL	6	1	38	36	25
CATTERICK	22	41	17	25	5
CHELTENHAM *	7	19	19	12	11
CHEPSTOW	37	20	37	18	36
DONCASTER	21	3	16	30	1
EXETER	8	9	1	13	7
FAKENHAM	12	15	34	9	13
FOLKESTONE	9	30	3	5	33
FONTWELL	29	29	32	10	38
HAYDOCK *	42	40	31	40	18
HEREFORD *	13	18	28	19	14
HEXHAM	18	33	35	23	30
HUNTINGDON *	41	42	24	22	8
KELSO	32	16	6	20	16
KEMPTON	24	37	7	33	10
LEICESTER	15	11	26	39	29
LINGFIELD	25	12	NA	NA	42
LUDLOW	19	8	27	27	22
MARKET RASEN	36	9	9	28	24
MUSSELBURGH	2	17	15	6	31
NEWBURY *	39	43	36	16	40
NEWCASTLE *	17	27	5	34	27
NEWTON ABBOT	23	32	29	29	34
PERTH	33	38	14	11	21
PLUMPTON	4	6	8	21	12
SANDOWN *	27	26	42	37	41
SEDGEFIELD	10	27	41	28	26
SOUTHWELL	3	21	4	8	39
STRATFORD	34	22	22	4	23
TAUNTON	12	23	18	35	28
TOWCESTER	28	14	10	14	4
UTTOXETER	31	31	20	26	15
WARWICK	40	36	30	31	19
WETHERBY *	20	35	11	32	9
WINCANTON	5	2	13	3	20
WOLVERHAMPTON *	38	13	21	15	NA
WORCESTER	35	6	40	41	35
NB: Rank of 1 = highest number of fallers per fence faced					
* Courses that have been reported in racing literature to have stiff fences					

Wincaton, Exeter, and Ayr emerged as the courses that consistently proved difficult to complete. In the main, the position of each course in the ranking order was stable; Aintree (Mildmay), Bangor, Fontwell, and Newton Abbot being good examples. In other cases such as that of Aintree's National course, a strong trend was interrupted by a period of two seasons when the fences seemed to prove softer. The tracks that are supposed to boast stiff fences (indicated by asterisks on the table) do not necessarily seem to witness an increased regularity of fallers- Sandown and Newbury being clear examples. Interestingly, the frequency of fallers at some of the courses changed markedly over time. For example, Perth's fences appear to be growing stiffer whereas Cartmel's obstacles represented a lesser challenge in 2003-2004 than they did during the first two seasons of the analysis. This variability flies in the face of the commonly held view that the stiffness of the fences at a given track is a stable trait.

THE TWO TRIBES

The schism between the supporters of National Hunt and flat racing was delightfully exposed by the anthropologist Kate Fox. Most serious backers would tell you that the flat offers more opportunities for profitable betting by virtue of stronger markets, a greater number of races, and the draw bias among other factors. Indeed, it has often been said that jump racing provides less of an edge for the backer to exploit. Despite these admonitions, I love both codes and regard the proclivity to attach oneself to either clan as idiocy. In particular, it has become all too fashionable to deride National Hunt racing. I wonder if individuals who indulge in this censure are suffering from what Freud might have referred to as 'hurdle envy'. One of the beautiful qualities of racing in this country is the way in which the flat and jumps seasons compliment each other. For once in life you can have your cake and eat it.

As we approach the conclusion of the flat season and the festering hype that accompanies the Breeders Cup, the first National Hunt races of value emerge like a welcome renaissance. However, by the time the Grand National has been won and lost in April, the flat season beckons once more with the promise of perfect summer afternoons under azure skies set to a soundtrack of thundering hooves.

There are senses in which National Hunt racing compares very favourably to its counterpart. The athleticism and grace of the jumping horse are unparalleled within the sport. Furthermore, one can follow the careers of jumpers over many years and their reappearance each autumn is like a reunion. There is a sprinkling of chasers in action today that were racing in juvenile hurdles in the mid-1990s. The superlative jumpers have the chance to claim multiple championships at Cheltenham and return each year to defend their crowns. Conversely, on the flat, a new batch of equine progeny rolls off the breeding production lines every season. Due to the increased stud value of colts whose record remains unblemished, the very best three-year-olds of each generation are typically retired to stud, never to be seen again on a racetrack. What would football be like if every successful team was retired at the end of each season to be replaced with unknown players? At the highest level, flat racing has become the neglected child of the billion-pound global bloodstock industry. The dominance of breeding collectives such as Coolmore and Godolphin has made the sport top-heavy.

Just as racing careers can be over too quickly on the flat, so can the races. Terry Ramsden, a stockbroker from Enfield who lost £57 million to the bookmakers in three years, once quipped that the flat is a "quicker death" when compared to the jumps. If on the other hand you are a winner then the measured build-up of a competitive National Hunt race can prove far more gratifying. There is time to savour every nuance of the contest and the duels that can take place over the final two or three obstacles are heart stopping.

The National Hunt calendar draws towards a celebrated zenith at the Cheltenham Festival, which yields a panoply of championship races. Hence, there is a balance and almost narrative flow to the season. By contrast, the flat season's most valuable prizes are spilt over the summer months in kaleidoscopic disarray. The timing of the 1000 and 2000 Guineas constitutes a prime example. Should we suffer a late spring, it becomes simply impossible for trainers whose horses remain on these shores over the winter to bring their charges to peak fitness by early May. Furthermore, the soft ground will decimate opportunities for a preparation race. The guineas are the three-year-old championship races at the distance of a mile and yet the runners are still rapidly maturing at the time of the race. Indeed, the colts and fillies that are destined to become the best milers in time will not have developed the requisite maturity to endure the distance until much later in the season. There are prestigious mile races open to these horses later in the summer, but the result of the Guineas is the one that will be recorded for posterity.

National Hunt racing is especially vulnerable to accusations of animal cruelty due to the number of injuries and fatalities that befall horses in the act of jumping. The political climate regarding the welfare of animals is changing and one encounters an increasing number of people who regard jump racing as cruel. There have long been undercurrents of protest that find their focus in the Grand National. Indeed, it might not be long before the supporters of National Hunt racing are forced to defend their sport against the same level of reproach that hunting itself has received. Someone who profits from betting on the results of jump races should not deny the dangerous reality that horses and jockeys face. It is hard not to be affected by incidents such as the death of Valiramix during the 2002 Champion Hurdle; a

Valiramix

tragic hero if ever there was one. Fortunately, initiatives in veterinary research, such as the programme at Liverpool University, are exploring ways in which fractures can be prevented. In my own opinion, the overall benefits to humans and horses that are derived from racing outweigh the health risks that are taken by jockeys and their mounts, but those risks should still be comprehensively addressed.

The hazards of the jumping game may lead owners and trainers to favour the potentially more profitable all-weather alternative. Notably, every one of the new racecourses that is being proposed in this country is an all-weather track. Venerable courses such as Newmarket, Kempton, and Newbury have all obtained permission to host all-weather fixtures in 2006, while the new racecourse at Great Leighs in Essex will also host racing on an artificial surface. It is no exaggeration to say that the structure of British horseracing is in a state of flux and the precise future of National Hunt racing is far from certain. However, it is uplifting to reflect that there was a dark time in the mid-1970s when Aintree was threatened with extinction; a notion that seems barely credible today. And that is an encouraging thought.

CHAPTER 21
Selection Systems

When you sit down to analyse a race on which you may wish to bet, you are presented with a plethora of variables relating to the runners: age, previous performances, preferences for race conditions etc. You are also aware of factors that pertain to the conditions of the race: the going, race distance, course and so on. Based on your acquired knowledge, you will form an opinion regarding the likely outcome of the race. What you will have done in the space of a few minutes is a testament to the complexity of the human brain. This only becomes apparent when one tries to represent the process of selection in an abstract way; it defies description. No computer programme or transparent system of reasoning could emulate the dynamism and infinite nuance that your mind applies to the problem of finding winners. The thought process is organic and therefore it adapts; less like a machine and more like a garden in which ideas grow. By comparison, a systematic approach to betting is rigid and inhibited by pre-ordained constraints and relative simplicity.

A rule-based system involves the imposition of rigid selection criteria such as backing top-weights in nursery races. The system may be further refined by adding additional constraints, for example, only betting when the going is good-to-soft. However, most simplistic systems lack potency when pitted against the sheer complexity of a horse race. The rule-based system is blind and does not censor for the changing circumstances that are inherent in racing. Relying entirely on a rigid systematic approach is like convicting the defendant after hearing only the first witness. The reason that such approaches prevail is enshrined in the ironic title of Nick Mordin's book *Winning Without Thinking*. Such a notion ministers to the indolence in everyone but the truth is that winners do a lot of thinking. All that you will achieve from betting without thinking are debts.

There are more sophisticated techniques than merely selecting horses that fulfil a certain criterion. One such method would be to award points on a scale reflecting the horse's merit in various respects. For example, a horse that won its last race might be awarded 10 points, and one less point could be given for every place behind the winner (i.e., 2nd place = 9 points, 3rd place = 8 points etc.). Points might also be allotted in a mechanistic manner using a statistic such as an ability rating. Alternatively, you might decide to make a subjective judgement and award a score based on your own appraisal of the horse. In either case, points could be assigned according to several different criteria. This process would result in an overall rating that would allow you to compare each runner in the race. In order to increase the sensitivity of this method, the different criteria could be weighted. For example, you may feel that the ability rating of a horse is a far more significant consideration than the animal's fitness and thus award each runner points out of 20 for ability and points out of 10 for fitness. Hence, it is possible to skew the overall rating in order to reflect your personal estimation of the relative importance of different selection criteria.

If you choose to construct a rating by adding together the scores that you award a horse according to various criteria, then you are making the assumption that these criteria are independent from each other. But what if they interact? For example, let us assume that we are using two variables to assess a runner's prospects of winning a race. The first of these two is the horse's preference for different types of going while the second is the horse's best speed rating, which in this case is very high. If the runner in question has shown a marked preference for heavy ground yet she is running today on firm ground then her previous speed figures will be irrelevant. Hence, to merely add the scores relating to these two variables together would produce a meaningless result because they interact. Depending on the particular circumstances, different variables assume greater or lesser importance and react with each other in different ways. Such considerations are reflective of the type of reasoning that an astute bettor employs when he examines the form of each runner in a forthcoming race. A myriad of clues is available, but the shrewd backer is able to discern which of them have relevance under the prevailing conditions. Hence, what is really required is a different system for every race and every horse.

COMPUTERS AND NEURAL NETWORKS

Of course, there are more sophisticated ways to combine and score variables than merely assigning points for various criteria and calculating an overall rating. The last decade or so has seen breathtaking advances in the computer modelling techniques that have been applied to the problem of forecasting the results of horse races. These approaches extend the principle of systematic selection a step further because they incorporate vast numbers of variables and use relatively advanced mathematical techniques to assign probabilities to each runner in a race. One encounters the view among many backers that computers have become a false god in the betting domain. Without question, the utility of computer-based prediction systems depends on the intelligence of the person typing in the commands. The computer is merely a tool that permits one to make calculations and handle data far faster than one could on paper. Thus, in the hands of the right individual, a computer can be used to develop and test ever more refined techniques. Consequently, computers can provide what all backers seek: the famed advantage over other bettors known as an 'edge'.

Those who dismiss the relevance of computers in betting are wrong to do so and their ignorance and incredulity create opportunities for others. I know this because I have encountered computer-based approaches that yield a robust profit over long periods of time. Hence, I made the decision at a very early stage to incorporate computers into my betting strategy and it has proved to be the correct one. In fact, I would go as far as to suggest that, as their use becomes even more commonplace, computers will become essential to profitable betting; without one, you are at a huge disadvantage. Although I had scant knowledge of computers to begin with, I felt confident that I would be able to learn about them. I was helped by the fact that I grew up in the late eighties and early nineties, at a time when personal computers were becoming readily affordable. Consequently, I followed the trend of playing computer games and writing simple programmes. Those of you who have ever owned a Spectrum or Commodore will know what I mean. Does the following ring a bell!?

```
>10 PRINT "HELLO"
>20 GOTO 10
>RUN
```

Fortunately, I seemed to possess a flair for programming and began to tackle more advanced projects. This career finally culminated in expulsion from the computer club at my secondary school when I found a way to infiltrate the school's network of BBC micros and afford myself all sorts of privileges that I had no right to. On one memorable day I managed to foreshorten the final period of the day by activating the school's bell prematurely. Understandably, the senior computer teacher, who resembled an ageing rocker in a tweed jacket, banned me for life because I represented a "threat to the security of the network." I then forgot about computers entirely, as this was the moment I discovered girls. I dropped all my computer classes and when I arrived at University some four years later, the personal computer had changed beyond all recognition and it was as if I had never seen one in my life. Little did I know that my aimless adolescent adventures in programming would return to play such an important part in my adult life.

This book is not about the specifics of using computers in betting. Nevertheless, I would like to provide a snapshot of the techniques I use so as to give an overview of what's involved. In order to perform the various analyses that feature in this book, I used raw data that I loaded into Microsoft Excel, which is a spreadsheet application. In this particular case, I exported the data I needed from the electronic formbook that I use. There are generally two types of dataset: one relating to the characteristics of each runner (age, finishing position, ratings etc.) and another relating to the conditions of each race (prize money, grade, going etc.). It is possible to write and operate programmes in Excel that are known as 'macros'. Hence, I taught myself how to write macros so that I could perform various operations with the raw data. For example, I wrote a macro that sifted through the set, identified which horses had won their previous race, and calculated the profit that would have resulted from backing them. A basic level of mathematical ability is required to manipulate the data in the way that is necessary but I am no mathematician. There is no special benefit to be derived from applying arcane and bewildering formulae for complexity's sake. In fact when I have tried to incorporate relatively advanced procedures (polynomial regression, structural equation modelling, and other similar gobbledygook) the results have been utterly hopeless. The simplest approaches really are the best.

Most computer modelling techniques in the betting domain follow a similar principle. Variables such as the ones presented in the previous chapters are coded so that their values are expressed along a similar scale (e.g., between 0 and 1). These variables are known as 'predictors' because they are used to predict the outcome of the race that is being analysed. The predictor variables relating to each horse are then subjected to a series of mathematical operations in order to produce an output variable, which is like a rating that expresses the likelihood of the horse winning. However complex the modelling technique, we are still limited by its inflexibility and failure to cope with changing circumstances. Nevertheless, work in the field of artificial intelligence has yielded a technology known as neural networks, which partially circumvents this problem by mimicking the learning capabilities of our brains. A neural network consists of a series of interconnected 'nodes', each of which is represented by a numerical value (see Figure 1).

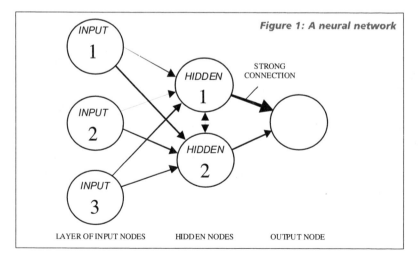

Figure 1: A neural network

The predictor variables such as previous form and speed ratings determine the values of the input nodes. These values are then transmitted to a 'hidden' layer of nodes via connections of differing 'strength' that can render the values greater or smaller. The value of each hidden or output node is determined by the sum of the inputs it receives. If you provide a neural network with a series of past results in the form of predictor variables (inputs) and an appropriate output variable such as the finishing position of the horse, it will 'learn' to predict the output variable from the input variables. Every time inputs are fed into the network an output is produced. This output is then compared with the actual output, i.e., the finishing position of the horse, and the strength of the connections between the various nodes are adjusted so that the network's 'prediction' is as close as possible to the actual outcome of the race. After a network has been 'trained' with many examples, its outputs begin to reflect the pattern of results it has been exposed to. Thus, the network has 'learned' the relationship between the predictor variables and the output variable and can therefore be 'queried' with new data to elicit an output when the result is not known, i.e., a race that has not yet been run. A neural network is so called because the nodes and their interconnections represent the neurones and synapses of the brain; and it is this similitude that allows the network to mimic the dynamic process of human thought.

Neural networks have been utilised in many artificial intelligence applications such as predicting the weather and anticipating credit-card fraud. Possibly the first instance of their use in predicting the results of horse races occurred in 1990. A professional backer named Don Emmons used an affordable neural network computer programme to predict the performances of horses running at the Detroit racecourse in Michigan. The strike rate of his bets in the 1990 flat season was an unworldly 78%. On these shores, the man who is associated with neural networks in the racing domain is Dr. Peter May, the author of the book that I referred to in the introduction. I have used neural networks since reading Dr. May's book in 2000 and the results have been excellent.

The technicalities relating to the development and training of neural networks are beyond the province of this book. However, I hope that I have provided you with an insight into their utility. Needless to say, the results that you obtain will only be as good as the data that you use. If one selects inappropriate variables and prepares them in a less than thoughtful manner before inputting them, the results produced by the network will be meaningless; garbage in, garbage out, as the sceptics would say. In order to produce good results a lot of diligence is required. A neural network will certainly not detect a profitable pattern in any accumulation of data you care to provide it with. Even so, success is attainable. I trained a network with just four predictor variables that has elicited a very robust profit over the last four flat seasons in my chosen area of operations: non handicap races for three-year-olds. The predictor variables that I used were all to be found in the *Racing Post* although I had to code (prepare) them prior to input.

SYSTEMS IN PRACTICE

Because systems offer a consistent method of making selections, it is easy to assume that they yield consistent results – the holy grail of every backer and the antidote to uncertainty. If you can believe in a system then you can avoid the necessity of believing in yourself. Despite the limitations of systematic approaches, they are still very popular with certain sections of the betting public. Hence, I will play devil's advocate and outline some of the advantages that apply to systems and the considerations that should be made when developing and testing them.

The inflexibility of systems is a curse but it may also be a blessing. It is highly important to be consistent in your betting approach. Emotion can often impinge upon your ability to apply your own principles in the heat of battle. Imagine that you had to place an enormously large bet equivalent to your annual salary. Would you approach the wager with the same nonchalance you show when betting with pocket change or would your judgement be affected? Human thought is very vulnerable to what psychologists call ironic mental processes. Research on that subject has demonstrated that one of the best ways to prevent yourself from sleeping is to 'try' and go to sleep. Similar thought patterns occur when betting; you can try so hard not be distracted by the size of your bet that this effort in itself distracts you and distorts your reasoning. It is not only the size of your bet that influences your pattern of thought; your recent run of results, level of confidence, and prevailing mood all intrude upon your mental activity. The application of a system promises to take the human element out of the equation.

"I've learned the lesson that the worst thing that can happen to a gambler is to let his recent losses or wins knock him off keel emotionally"
Andrew Beyer, noted American backer

Another benefit that is associated with systems is the facility to test the performance of your method on past results. If I can demonstrate that the approach I am considering produced a healthy profit in three separate seasons over the course of thousands of races then I can have increased confidence that I will be successful when I apply it. It is essential to develop and then test a system with separate datasets in order to ascertain that it is generalisable. Envisage that I considered a season's racing results and I focussed on two simple variables: speed ratings and the trainer's SR%. If I investigated every possible combination of the two variables then I would probably uncover a synthesis of them that would yield a profit over the season. I may find that backing all horses with the highest speed figures in their respective races and a trainer whose SR was between 10 and 15% would lead to positive returns. However, I would be a fool to subsequently use my system to make selections and bet on them. There is little underlying sense behind this system, it simply happened to fit the pattern of results which was present in the data that I used to develop it. Remember that a handful of results can completely alter the success of an approach over the course of an entire season.

The analysis I undertook of profitable stalls in Chapter 18 was a good example of a thoroughly researched system. Firstly, I based the analysis on the premise of the draw bias. Secondly, I only considered stalls that had produced a consistent profit over several separate seasons. When developing and testing a system or approach, try not to pull too many strings in order to force a solution that returns handsome profits. You will have to refine the system to some extent as a matter of course but if you bend over backwards in the attempt then you will find that your method generalises poorly.

Even if you are testing your approach on two separate datasets, there is a chance that you are merely converging on a solution that best fits the unique characteristics of the data that you are using and would thus generalise poorly if you introduced a third set of data. If the system that you have developed is built on sound foundations then it will produce a robust profit regardless of any fine-tuning that you undertake. To return to the analogy with science that I used at the start of the book, it is important to develop a hypothesis and then set out to test this using available data before revision and further testing. Most successful systems are based on very intelligent but simple ideas and, as with scientific investigation, a creative spark is vital to ignite the process of discovery.

Experience will reveal that when you operate systems, the profits and strike rates never quite match the levels you established during testing. You must learn to accept this depreciation and make allowances for it when you are planning your betting strategy. One of the pitfalls of developing and testing systems is the sheer perspicacity that is required. Like all that is valuable, successful betting approaches are hard to find. Thus, on many of the occasions when you believe you have discovered a profitable pattern, you will have made an error. Your powers of judgement will always be susceptible to the phenomenon that Michael Adams described in his critique of selection systems:

"Pattern recognition is a basic feature of human intelligence. So it's not surprising if there's often a real feeling of euphoria following the discovery of a hidden pattern or equation, which can apparently make sense of what was formerly a mass of seemingly unconnected data. All the more so, if it also seems to offer a way of making easy money."

I can remember an occasion when I decided to investigate the effects of dividing my stake across the two most highly rated selections in each race. After running an analysis I found that the profit levels over several seasons' worth of data were breathtaking and I was struck with the conviction that I had discovered the key to the mythical bookmakers' safe. I felt a pang of sympathy for my old adversaries Ladbrokes and William Hill as I contemplated that my superior weaponry would render their defeat at my hands inevitable. But this condolence subsided after a second or so and I leapt from my chair, proceeding to dance around the bedroom as if celebrating a goal that I had scored. The frenzy of jubilation reached a glorious crescendo as I pranced about on the bed like a rutting stag, wagging my index finger at the computer in the infamous style of Dennis Taylor. Then a thought occurred to me and I clambered down from the bed and checked a couple of lines in the computer programme that I had written to display the results. Due to a mistake that I had made, the programme was failing to deduct the losses that occurred when neither of the two selections was successful in a race! Since that day, I have discovered numerous other apparent goldmines. A couple of these have even stood up to scrutiny. But I have not danced on any beds. The moral of the story is never underestimate the power of denial. When you are working with computers you must be prepared to double-check every last calculation with the rigour of an air-traffic controller. In my case, a mistake buried in one line of a computer programme could cost me thousands of pounds.

It is quite possible to compile odds based on the ratings that your chosen method produces and compare these values to the prices that are on offer. Although this is a simple enough procedure, the results are typically worthless; one finds oneself comparing apples and oranges. Most systems produce ratings that censor for a very limited number of factors, whereas the actual odds on offer represent a numerical composite of everything that is known about the horse in question. Hence, any discrepancy between the odds you have compiled and the ones that are available in the ring can generally be attributed to a factor that has not been properly considered in your framework of selection. If you have ever tried to create your own tissue of prices based on ratings, you will have noticed that it appears distorted and unnatural when compared to its genuine equivalent. It is possible to use mathematical formulae to massage the prices into a more plausible shape, but the effect is cosmetic.

Although the prices on offer in the betting market do correspond well to each horse's actual probability of success (see Chapter 5), the prices also reflect the subjective value of expert opinion, the fickle behaviour of the betting public, and the machinations of bookmakers. The assignation of probability to the event of a horse winning a race is prohibitively difficult. Indeed, I have only ever encountered one mathematical technique that produced odds which outperformed the market.

Many commercially available computer applications are accompanied by claims that accurate odds are generated; however, in practice they fall a long way short of this goal.

The method I use to interpret my ratings is disarmingly simple but it has been subjected to extensive testing and produced very respectable results. I merely back the top-rated selection if the price on offer lies within the 4-1 to 8-1 bracket that I favour. Research has shown me that this is the band of prices that yields the best returns for all of my different betting approaches. If the system that I am employing does not yield a clear selection then I refrain from betting; once more, my past results indicate that this abstinence is wise. One needs to specialise in specific domains of racing (e.g., non-handicap novice hurdle races) rather than attempting to develop an 'ecumenical' approach that can be used across the board. Although it has been done, designing a systematic approach that produces a slight profit when applied to all races is extremely difficult. The separate domains in racing are like sports within a sport and it will always prove more profitable to specialise. However, if you become too focussed then the danger is that you will merely be reacting to anomalous trends because the sample size you are working with is too small.

In the foregoing chapters of this book, I have demonstrated that certain variables are of more relevance in some domains of racing than in others. A good example is the performance ratings that are produced by private handicappers. These ratings appears to be a key consideration in non-handicap races for juvenile runners but nearly irrelevant in handicaps. It is important to narrow your focus onto a specific type of race and choose appropriate variables. For example, if you focus on races for two-year-olds then speed ratings and the trainer's strike rate would probably be the most important considerations.

The results obtained by systems can usually be improved by eliminating bets in certain types of races. For example, the neural network system that I referred to earlier based on non-handicap races for three-year-olds performed poorly under the following circumstances:

- Early or late season (March, April, September, October)
- Large fields (over 13 runners)
- Selling or claiming races
- Soft or heavy ground
- Low prize-money (under £3k first prize)

If you eliminate any categories of races or types of horses then it is imperative that you have a sound reason for doing so. If selections in a particular category yield unfavourable results then this might be due to a statistical aberration. Hence, if your selections perform poorly in August but not in September or July then you should question why this is. Look for smooth trends in the data that reveal an underlying effect rather than arbitrary peaks and troughs which could signify nothing. Once again, sample size is a very important consideration. Experience tells me that a system which has produced a profit of 25p per pound staked over the course of 300 races will generally outperform one that has generated a profit of 50p over 100 races. Statistically, there will be a greater chance of losing money when following the latter approach.

Just to confuse matters still further, it is worth bearing in mind that many systems rely on an underlying factor that changes over time. The betting market is a very reflexive mechanism and prices will shift to account for a successful method. Somewhat depressingly, I refer to this principle as 'profit evaporation' and its effect is particularly acute when you are following a method that other backers or layers might conceivably be utilising. Indeed, once a certain system becomes publicised then a domino effect occurs as it rapidly becomes common knowledge. For these reasons, it is imperative to make hay while the sun shines.

Knowing when to jump ship is a particularly hard skill to learn as there is always a temptation to hang on for more profits. The necessities of testing your system with a large enough sample and avoiding the pitfalls of profit evaporation seem to oppose each other. Hence, a balance must be sought between the two. On a more encouraging note, it is important to remember that most systems are developed and tested with starting prices. Hence, you will have a good chance of boosting profits through expeditious betting. You may be forgiven for thinking that once you have researched a profitable method, all you need do is sit back and watch like an impassive observer as your winnings accumulate. Not so; you will be fortune's toy just like any other backer. When your method is producing profit you will feel like a sweepstake winner and your friends will call you 'butter' because you are on a roll! However, when things start to go awry, you will feel like a sailor on a doomed ship that is heading inexorably for ruinous rocks. Ever remember cycling as a child and closing your eyes for a couple of seconds just to cheat fate? That's what using a system is like; riding in the dark.

You will need stoic confidence to continue following a method that appears to be flying on one engine. The worst eventuality is a partial commitment; you might as well not bother at all. If you decide to follow a system then you have to support it sickness and in health. The ignominy of realising that you would have made a profit had you stuck to your guns is the worst way to lose money because you know that you got the hard part right. You feel like a striker who lost his marker, ghosted into space, and then missed the simple tap in that would have won the game. In order to be aware of what you are letting yourself in for, examine the past performance of your system and observe the losing runs and patterns of results that you can expect.

One of the difficulties attached to following systems is the fact that you often find yourself backing runners that your instincts tell you to avoid. There is a very strong temptation to exercise a prerogative and veto some of your system's selections. In theory, this hybrid approach to betting would appear to offer the best of both worlds. In practice, you must exercise caution when interpreting the output of a systematic approach. Profitable systems generally identify favourably-priced runners that are overlooked by the betting public. Hence, part of the logic of such systems is to select horses that appear to be poor bets when viewed through the lens of conventional wisdom.

Cautionary tales abound and I have certainly had costly experiences of meddling with the selections generated by a system. I followed one such method during a recent flat season and although the level of profit and strike rate that it generated were a little below my expectations, the results were respectable. There were 81 runners of which 15 won at average odds of 11/2 whilst the profit per pound staked was 22p. In my wisdom, I saw fit to exclude what I felt were the weaker selections and back the remaining 53 runners. I was rewarded for my efforts with a derisory profit of £122 after staking a total of £10,600! Embarrassingly, the 28 selections that I had passed on returned a profit of 39p per pound staked. This example is somewhat extreme but it makes the point admirably. As you become more adept at applying systems then you might grant yourself some latitude in interpreting their results, but caution should be your North Star. If the system in question has successfully produced a profit over several seasons without your assistance then there is no need to be greedy!

BETTING SYSTEMS: A CONCLUSION

However systematic your approach, you will never be able to completely abdicate responsibility for making selections. What happens if your system yields three selections in the same race? Maybe you have resolved to never bet at odds-on and your selection is hovering precariously between evens and 10/11. Under such circumstances, it is incumbent upon you to call heads or tails. A systematic selection method can't place your bets for you. If the system you follow fails to produce a profit then you are the one that will lose money, so why disadvantage yourself by disabling the most effective tool that you have at your disposal- your mind.

Betting CHAPTER 22

RECORDS

You might have noticed that at several points in this book I have referred to analysing one's own betting records. This process goes hand in hand with taking your betting seriously. A backer without betting records doesn't even know if he has been successful or not. Can you imagine the football premiership without a league table or a cricket match without a scoreboard? The scrutiny of your records provides you with a framework to understand and develop your performance.

Establish a format for your records and decide which information you are going to include and in what form. I keep my records on a computer spreadsheet in a very minimal format that facilitates review. The advantage of the spreadsheet is that it performs all necessary calculations automatically and informs me at a glance what my strike rate and profit level is for various types of bet. If your notes are scrawled in a haphazard fashion in some exercise book then sifting through them can become like deciphering the Dead Sea scrolls. Decide which information you are likely to refer back to in the future and make sure that it is prominently displayed in your records.

STAKING AND MONEY MANAGEMENT

Those perennial questions! You should think in the long term when you devise a staking plan. I review my stakes at the start of every season (flat and National Hunt). My aim is to make a profit over a season of betting. Hence, it is logical to adjust my stakes according to the same time frame. The level of your stakes is dependent on the size of your betting bank; a sum that should be kept entirely separate from the remainder of your assets. I use a current account that I opened for this very purpose. However adept you are, there is still a small chance that you will loose your entire betting bank, so it must only ever be a part of your overall capital. Hence, if the unthinkable happens and you lose your betting bank, you will be able to 'stay alive'.

Once your betting bank has been determined, you must consider the pattern of results that you are likely to face. Your own records and the typical odds about your selections will enlighten you as to the strike rate you can expect. For example, I know that my strike rate will vary from between 20 to 25% over time. The conventional procedure is to set your stakes to such a level that would accommodate the longest losing run you could reasonably expect without facing the dissolution of your betting bank. However, what if you encountered two of these losing runs interspersed by a single winner? What one is trying to censor for, is the maximum loss that is probable over the course of your betting period. Examine Graph 9 and note the fluctuation of the bank that I used for bets in maiden races during the last flat season. Each white point on the line represents a bet of £100.

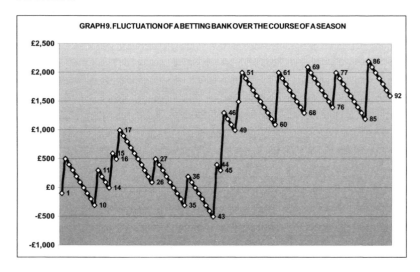

As you will be able to see from my example, the longest losing run I suffered was eight bets. Yet between bets number 17 and 43 I lost £1,500. Had I commenced at bet number 17 instead of bet 1, I would have required a bank of some £1,600 at the very least. The greatest positive flux in my betting bank occurred between bets number 43 and 86; had I bet for this period of time then I would have netted a profit of £2,750. Michael Adams performed a series of computer simulations that revealed the likelihood of doubling or busting a betting bank over many sequences of races. His results indicated that, with stakes set to 5% of the opening betting bank, a strike rate of 20%, and a profit level of 20p per pound staked (almost the exact parameters of the above example), I would have a 79% chance of doubling my bank over 100 races, but a 16% chance of blowing it all together. If I decreased my stake to 2.5% of the opening bank, I would have only a 3% chance of losing all my money, but a smaller chance of doubling the bank over 100 races (63%). Seen in this light, even setting the level of your stake is a bet in itself.

In specifying your stake, you walk a tightrope between busting your betting bank and failing to produce sufficient profit. It depends on the strike-rate that you generate and the levels of profit you anticipate, but if you follow my example, then your stake would be somewhere between 2.5% and 5% of your opening betting bank depending on what level of risk you are comfortable with. Hence, if your initial bank stood at £2,000 then your stakes would be somewhere between £50 and £100. The lower the level of profit that you expect to generate in the long run, the more cautious you must be with your staking.

However, no adjustments can compensate for poor selections or the failure to obtain favourable prices. Thus, the goal of your staking decision is not to magically turn a series of poor bets into a slight profit, but to enable yourself to make the best profit possible while managing the risk of losing your bank should the pattern of results turn against you. A further dimension of staking is the emotional impact of betting with large sums; an issue that was discussed in the previous chapter. Every backer has a comfort zone and it is essential not to exceed yours otherwise your betting performance will be affected.

What level of profit can you expect? Well, I aim to make a profit of 20% on turnover (a return of 20p per pound staked). Fabled backers from the annals of betting history such as Alex Bird aimed for around 4% based on an annual outlay of £2 million (1950's money!) although his winnings touched 35% in some years. Bird's contemporary Phil Bull aimed for around 8% profit. The developers of a well-known and proven computer modelling technique produce around 5% profit and claim that it is very unlikely one will make more than 10%. Nick Mordin famously proved that it is possible to make a living from betting and wrote a book relating his exploits. His profit over a six-month period approached 200%, which he confessed was the result of much good fortune. Alan Potts wrote in his first book that he aimed to achieve a profit of 10%. However, by the time he wrote his second book three years later, he was reporting profits of well over 30%. Much depends on your initial capital and your ambitions. Obviously, if your bank is large enough to finance revolutions, then a 5% profit will do very nicely, but why are you betting in the first place if you have all that money!? In the time-honoured style of such books, I should attempt to dissuade you from endeavouring to bet for a living. However, the figures that I have provided you with above should indicate how much capital is required to undertake such a task.

STAKING SYSTEMS

I would prefer not to dignify the quackery of staking systems by introducing them here. However, their popularity forbids me this easy option. In almost every good book I have ever read about betting there are thorough explanations of why level stakes are the preferable option. Some of those books include whole chapters that have been devoted to testing various staking adjustment systems against level stakes to prove that they are ineffective. I could do likewise, but I won't for the same reason that I don't need to provide copious tables, charts, and examples to explain why you should not run under a bus or streak at a close relative's funeral. The pattern of results that you experience (i.e., the dispersion of winners during a period of betting) is entirely random. Consequently, to adjust your stake in reaction to wins and losses is to completely misunderstand the nature of betting. For similar reasons, the alteration of your stake in proportion to the fluctuating size of your betting bank is naïve, and those who have commended this course of action in the racing media are doing backers a disservice. If you return to the above graph depicting the fluctuation of a betting bank over the course of a season you will understand why. If it were possible to be absolutely sure that profits would follow in a consistent manner then staking as a percentage of your betting bank would serve as a quicker way to increase your capital. However, even when a profitable system is followed, the pattern of results may still prove very uneven. For this reason, it is best to revise stakes at periodic intervals (e.g., every 50 bets) even if one confidently expects profit.

I think you will agree that one faces enough uncertainty already in betting without multiplying it with arbitrary staking systems. The aims of such procedures can be properly accomplished by setting the level of your stakes in the way that I have described. The only factors that you need consider are the size of your initial betting bank, your strike rate, your estimated level of profit, and the length of the period over which you are betting (number of bets). Thus, you make a personal decision regarding how much risk you wish to take in order to increase your probability of making a profit.

DIFFERENT STAKES FOR DIFFERENT BETTING APPROACHES

I will own that I have simplified the picture of staking somewhat because I have based my advice on the premise of backing runners whose prices fall within a specific range (i.e., 4/1 to 8/1). If you choose to back runners across the continuum of prices ranging from odds-on favourites to longshots then the situation becomes slightly more complex. For example, you might have wondered what level of stakes I use when I am laying horses as opposed to backing them. In fact, I maintain a separate betting bank for each of the different approaches that I am using at any one time. For example, during the flat season I use three banks: one for laying, one for the bets in maiden races selected by my neural network, and one for my own selections in group races. I trisected my betting bank in this way because I felt it likely that I would experience different levels of success with the varying approaches that I use. Because I enjoy greater returns from laying, I concentrate a larger proportion of my capital and energy on this avenue of betting. Accordingly, I use a higher level of stakes when laying as opposed to backing, principally because the anticipated strike rate is so much higher (around 58%).

If the price that you are willing to accept about a horse varies greatly (e.g., 1/10 to 33/1) then the strike rate and profit you achieve when backing longer-priced selections will differ from that which you record when backing favoured horses. For example, you would not want to place exactly the same stake on a 1/5 chance as you would on a 20/1 outsider. Because longshots generally yield poorer returns and lower strike rates than favourites, the orthodox decision would be to adopt a variable stakes approach as described earlier in this book. Hence, you would back each horse to *return* a certain amount if it was successful. Although variable staking represents a fair rule of thumb for inexperienced backers who are unlikely to make a profit, a more sophisticated approach is called for if you take your betting seriously. In my experience, the more proficient a backer becomes, the more likely it is that he will yield his greatest profits from the bets he strikes at longer odds. Such wagers provide him with the greatest edge he is able to achieve over the betting public. If you don't believe me, then examine the records of professional backers that are available in books such as this one. If your longer-priced selections (over 10/1) do show the healthiest profit, would you want them to carry the smallest stakes!? This is why records of your betting performance are so important. If you learn that you are not making a profit when backing horses that are priced in a certain bracket (e.g., Evens to 3/1), then you should refrain from backing such runners altogether.

Bearing in mind all the aforementioned factors that you should consider when establishing the size of your stake, you should invest more in the selections that you typically produce the greatest profit with. I achieve this by using a larger betting bank and consequently higher stakes for my most successful approach, which is laying. You may ask why I don't just forget about backing horses altogether and concentrate on opposing them. I could answer by reminding you of an old adage … something about putting eggs in baskets, you know the one. I am no stockbroker, but I know that when people invest their money on the stock market, they generally have a portfolio of different shares rather than a holding in just one company. Hence, if your shares in Vodaphone head south for the winter (as mine did) then you still have Marks and Spencer or British Airways to balance your books. One is simply spreading the risk over different sectors of the market whose fortunes are not one and the same. In betting, the same principle applies: The potential for profit exists, but we need to do everything in our power to control the risks. Contrary to popular opinion, successful bettors are averse to risk. Hence, I would always prefer to operate three betting approaches that yield moderate levels of profit, rather than a single method which promises exceptional returns.

Generally, the more profitable a betting approach is, the more volatile is the pattern of results. Longshot bets are a case in point. Although many renowned backers enjoy large profits from their longer-priced selections, the strike rates is low and massive losing runs that stretch into months are quite common. Thus, even the most cavalier backers recognise the necessity of betting at more earthly prices in order to secure a relatively reliable income. One tactic is to use the winnings derived from bets placed at modest odds to fund the stakes for the longer-priced selections.

STAKING AND CONFIDENCE

There is one technique of altering one's stakes that is worthy of discussion. Successful backers often increase the level of their stake when they are especially confident about the selection they have made and feel that they have obtained a very favourable price. Indeed, there is a mathematical formula used by gambling syndicates and computer-based bettors which perfectly encapsulates this intuitive principle; a full account of the *Kelly Criterion* appears in *Winning Without Thinking*. In simple terms, the formula provides a precise method of determining your stake based on the confidence that you feel in a selection and the price that it is on offer. Logically, the highest stake would be carried by a runner that you felt was an almost certain winner yet started at very long odds. Conversely, if the horse that you chose to back started at odds which mirrored your own assessment then you would not bet as no advantage could be gained. In fact, what I have just described is precisely what experienced bettors do instinctively without the aid of a scientific calculator. The beauty of the Kelly Criterion is that it perfectly represents a process that occurs subliminally as we evaluate how much money to invest on a selection.

I believe that bettors who generate a consistent profit do so because they have a proven ability to back winners at favourable prices, i.e., instances when the runner in question is more likely to win a race than the available odds would suggest. Although it is never possible to truly ascertain when a favourable price has been obtained, the balance of a backer's results over time will provide evidence of his abilities in this respect. Indeed, the betting records of the most prolific backers that I have encountered confirm that the adjustment of stakes in this manner can yield returns which are superior to those derived from employing level stakes. The caveat is that if you are one of these backers then you shouldn't be reading a book about betting, you should be writing one. I have been studying racing and betting stratagems since I was a schoolboy and I don't feel confident enough to alter my stakes in the way that I have described. If you have been showing a robust profit with level stakes for years then it is possible that you have the skill to identify which of your selections are the most likely to generate a profit. The assumption being made is that even the selections about which you are least confident are profitable ones over time.

However prophetic you believe yourself to be, it is unwise to vary the size of your stake too greatly. For example, you should never let your largest stake be more than twice the value of your smallest stake. Tipsters who advise their disciples to stake on the basis of a points system with a 10-point maximum and a 1-point minimum are either gambling messiahs or they have got the balance quite wrong when it comes to staking. The one flaw in the Kelly Criterion when applied to betting is that it calculates stakes as a percentage of the overall betting bank. This means that in a situation in which you are totally confident you would be compelled to bet your entire betting bank on the result of one race! The eggs and basket expression is called for once again. Unless you have a reliable method of influencing the result of the race yourself then such high levels of confidence would be illusory. In fact, the very nature of racing is such that supreme confidence is generally unjustified even amongst the most prolific of backers. In my opinion, varying your stakes entails creating unnecessary additional risks and my best advice to you is to use level stakes without exception. If the decision regarding the stake has been made long in advance, then a lot of the anxiety is removed from the betting process. From a psychological point of view, it is nice to have a constant in an ever changing and uncertain world.

CONCERNING THE LONG-TERM MANAGEMENT OF BETTING CAPITAL

Once a period of betting ends, I review my financial position. For example, my bets in three-year-old maiden races start to dry up after the beginning of August and I therefore call a halt to proceedings. At this juncture, I have the choice of spending any winnings or reinvesting them by increasing the size of my subsequent betting banks. Although I may be operating as many as four betting banks simultaneously, I am not pedantic enough to use different bank accounts for each one. I have an accurate record of the level of each bank and therefore I know the amount of money in my betting account that pertains to each of the banks. I have only ever busted two betting banks, and on those occasions I merely stopped following that particular method and conducted a review.

I learned a salutary lesson in the first two months of the flat season in 2000, when a new technique that I had discovered in a book really ignited my betting performance. After three weeks of consistent and heavy profit I began to grow smug, and by the end of the first six weeks the winning was almost becoming a chore. I was so certain of my invincibility that I took the lion's share of my profit and bought a Jaguar (a car not a feline) with a pile of used notes. I spent the next few weeks cruising around West London in the style of a latter-day Arthur Daley, explaining the intricacies of my good fortune to anyone who was unfortunate enough to enter into conversation with me. This must have displeased the betting gods because they obviously decided to make an example of me. What happened to my betting after this could best be likened to a stock market crash. The upshot was that I was stuck with a pretentious car I couldn't really afford and the compunction to beg, steal, or borrow in order to prop up my emaciated betting bank. I switched to ageing Ford Orion and have to say that I found it to be a wonderful car!

FAVOURABLE PRICES

The aim of betting is not purely to find winners but to generate profit. In line with my approach to betting, I will be taking a long-term view. If you were given a single race to bet on and had to pick the winner to save your life, would you bet against the heavily odds-on favourite? Almost certainly not, I know I wouldn't. However, it should be your goal to make a profit over the course of the season and your betting should reflect this. The market provides an extremely reliable assessment of the probability that a given horse will win its race. Hence, it follows that if you want to find winners, you should back the horses with the shortest prices. If you follow this approach then you will make at worst a small loss. If, on the other hand, you want to generate a respectable profit then you have to look elsewhere and thus risk making a larger loss.

All the evidence that I have witnessed suggests that there is greater opportunity of striking bets at favourable prices when backing unfancied horses even though such runners yield relatively poor returns when they are followed blindly. Because of the market's accuracy, one must have superior knowledge in relation to the betting public in order to obtain a favourable price. The market mechanism ensures that the price you obtain about your selection will be partly determined by the betting activity that relates to other runners in the race, particularly those horses that head the market. Hence, it is often the case that you obtain a favourable price about your selection principally because others betted excessively on a particular fancied runner, most often the favourite. A good example of this effect would be the bias that the betting public demonstrates towards leading trainers and jockeys. The odds-compilers take this into account when they are forming the market and the short prices on offer serve to reinforce the prejudice that the punting masses hold.

VALUE

The central issue is that the search for favourable prices has become a betting religion known to its followers as 'value'. Such backers are so intent on finding value that they completely forget about whether a horse will win or lose, and their tents blow away in the wind, so to speak. The reason that value has become such a sacred cow is the prevalence of the topic in the betting media, particularly newspaper columns such as 'Pricewise' in the *Racing Post*. The punter who favours value for value's sake is like the shopper who purchases something because of a 'buy one get one free' offer, even if he has no need of the items in question. We have all ambled along supermarket aisles and been momentarily transfixed by the prospect of receiving a free tub of vanilla ice cream if we buy a frozen turkey. Indeed, seeking value in our inevitable transactions is part of human nature.

There was a time at the start of the last century when the betting markets were so inefficient that, in order to make a profit over time, all an adroit backer had to do was bet on every horse that seemed favourably priced. However, the accuracy of the modern betting market is fuelled by an intelligence network and information technology that would embarrass most small nations. To improve upon the market using the same publicly available information is a hopeless task. Of course there are individuals who are adept at assessing the relative chances of each horse in a race such as bookmakers, the official odds-compilers, and professional backers. However, most of us grossly underestimate the difficulty of the task. A pre-requisite of assessing a horse's prospects in a race is to evaluate each other competitor that the animal will face. In practice, it is very tempting to form opinions about a runner's chances without even considering its opponents.

The moment that odds become a selection criterion in their own right, then the balance is wrong. It is imperative to make your selection with as little initial regard to the probable market as possible. When I first began avoiding horses priced below 4/1, I would simply refrain from betting if I could not attain a price that was better than 4s in the ring. As a consequence of this temperance I encountered many races in which I could not bet and this grew frustrating. Over time, I began to pay too much attention to the projected starting prices and I started dismissing the prospects of fancied horses because I knew I wouldn't bet on them anyway. If I felt a horse was likely to start at odds of between 4/1 and 8/1 then I subconsciously favoured the animal and took a positive view of its prospects for success. Unsurprisingly, my bias resulted in a selection priced at 4/1 or over in almost every race. I have since mended my ways and learned a valuable lesson. The same mistake is made by those who back odds-on shots because they are reassured by the price and have formed the belief that the horse cannot lose before they have even looked at its record. At the other end of the scale, there are gamblers who back an outsider because it will provide them with a big return if it wins. The extent to which the term 'value' has been debased is apparent when you hear racing commentators routinely observing that any given horse with odds above 10-1 has a "value price". Hence, value has become synonymous with longer odds. When you hear the words "value price" or "bit of value", be as wary as a single person who is offered a blind date with somebody that has a "nice personality".

We all have some ability to estimate the relative chances of the runners in a race, otherwise we would have no basis to form selection decisions. The most prolific backers all lay similar claim to an ability to recognise favourable prices and their betting records are a fitting testament to that claim. However, moderation is a virtue

Rufus appeared to offer good value at 5000-1

in betting just as it is in all other things. Try not to attach too much value to 'value' or use it as a selection criterion in its own right. I know that around 80% of my bets lose. Hence, I do not expect to see my selection win but merely perform better than the market has predicted it will. Betting is ultimately an incredibly subjective domain and the only type of reality that I am interested in is my own. To say that it is impossible to ascertain the true chances of a horse winning its race is to miss the point entirely. Let me make it plain, if you select horses about which the bookmakers offer odds in the region of 6/1 and these runners frequently trouble the judge, then you will win money over time, pure and simple. How do I know this? Because I am doing it.

TYPES OF BET

If you have read books about betting before then I am sure that you already know I am going to advocate that you place single win bets. Very simply, the profit that bookmakers derive from other types of bet is higher and consequently they promote these more 'exotic' wagers with gusto. It depends on what your aims are, but if winning money is your concern then 'fun' bets involving multiple selections are about as entertaining as being mugged. If betting in a straightforward way is not challenging and exciting enough for you then go and take up an extreme sport, it will probably cost you less and you will be far more likely to achieve your goals. Betting is fraught with enough uncertainty and risk as it is without entering into lottery-style gambling and wagers that rely on a freakish string of occurrences. When you become so good that picking winners and making a profit are simply too easy then you might appreciate the additional challenge imposed by bets with multiple selections. Until then, the reasons to avoid such wagers are devastatingly simple: The latter stages of the bet have increasingly larger stakes running on to them and if your first selection is beaten then you fail to back the other horses that you selected.

CONCERNING EACH-WAY AND PLACE BETTING

Until recently, the only time that I had ever placed an each-way bet in my life was on the Grand National as a boy. A surprising number of the profitable backers that I have encountered or read about abhor each-way betting. Successful backers are highly confident in the selections that they make. Hence, to simultaneously back a horse to win and lose at the same time is thought to be a rather schizophrenic approach. It is the illogical bundling together of the win and place bets that deters astute backers. However, I have been forced to re-examine my contentions and take a more pragmatic view. If I double my stake and place each-way bets instead of win bets then I am effectively entering into an additional place bet on all my selections. I know that I am deriving a profit from my win bets. Hence, the real question is what sort of return would I be getting on the place part of these bets?

Most backers would tell you that the value offered by the each-way place fractions (e.g., a quarter of the odds for the first four places etc.) is dire. Many moons ago, the fractions were more generous and the now fabled 'each-way thieves' took advantage of this aberrant leniency on the part of the bookmakers. During the normal course of my research, I encountered an academic study undertaken by some American economists on the subject of each-way bets in the British betting markets. The findings indicated that small profits were possible from backing horses each-way under certain conditions. The reason for this is that the fractions which are used to determine the odds of a horse being placed are proportional to the win odds and provide inaccurate estimations of the actual chance that a horse will be placed.

Consider the following two hypothetical examples. The first race has eight runners, a 1/500 favourite, a 6/1 second favourite, and six rags priced at 250/1 (I said it was hypothetical!). The second example is also an eight-runner race but with eight co-favourites priced at odds of 6/1. The place odds for a 6/1 runner in an eight horse race are 6/5 (1/5 of 6/1). Although our 6/1 second favourite (in the first race) and our 6/1 co-favourites (in the second race) may have similar prospects of winning their respective races, a lobotomised monkey could tell you that the second favourite has a much higher chance of entering the first three places.

The American economists found that the best opportunities for exploiting this inaccuracy in the place odds came in handicap races with over 15 runners and hence four places. The runners to focus on had prices in the range of 11/4 to 5/1. In such instances, the positive returns from the place part of the bet were so great that they accounted for the negative returns derived from the win portion. Latterly, extensive research along the same lines by Michael Adams has revealed that, in certain types of races, each-way bets are likely to yield positive returns. In practice, seek races with very strong favourites, a second favourite that is priced at over 4/1, and a minimal number of horses with single-figure odds. Think of the extreme hypothetical example that I used. A horse's prospects of being placed in a given race are not necessarily related to its probability of winning. I am sure you can think of a horse that consistently fluffs his lines at short prices and is often in the frame but always finds one too good. One that comes to my mind is Venetia Williams' chaser Zabadi. The Irish-bred gelding succeeded in putting together a remarkable sequence of 28 races that included 13 second-places and a single win. Indeed, on 23 September 2000 at Plumpton, Zabadi achieved the dubious honour of his seventh runners-up prize in eight starts. Sadly, it costs a small fortune to rename a thoroughbred. Had it not been for this financial impediment, I might have been moved to write to Zabadi's owners and suggest that they should rename him 'never the bride'. Horses are not like human athletes and although they race, they may not be sufficiently motivated to make the effort required to win races. Equine psychologists might say that such animals are reluctant to assume leadership roles within a group!

A drawback is that many on-course bookmakers do not accept each-way bets. I am already limited because of the size of the stakes that I use. Hence, betting each-way proves to be a difficult proposition for me when I am on course. Both the tote place dividends and the betting exchange place odds do not adhere as closely to win prices as the place fractions offered by bookmakers. The diminutive size of the pools used for place betting with the tote and the level of deductions made are discouraging. Before I understood such issues properly, I thought that I had uncovered a very profitable mode of betting. I observed that hugely odds-on favourites sometimes yielded place dividends as large as their odds of winning with the bookmakers. For example, it is not uncommon to see a 1/5 favourite in a five horse race return a place dividend of £1.20 (equivalent to 1/5). I kept an eye open for such bets over a number of months although I was otherwise distracted by taking my GCSEs. However, when I eventually came to back one such fancy, I discovered to my horror that my paltry £40 stake had destroyed the dividend entirely and despite having picked the winner, I merely received my stake money back for my efforts.

When betting on the exchanges, I have found that the place prices on offer compare favourably to the fractions presented by the bookmakers. The bookies would laugh in your face if you wanted to strike a place-only bet at their odds and for good reason; the returns would be superior in most cases to those derived from win bets. Hence, place betting on the exchanges represents an excellent opportunity of generating profit. It depends on your approach to betting, but the advantages of a higher strike rate and reduced fluctuation in the level of your betting bank are obvious. Place betting assuages the prospect of a confidence-decimating run of losers that will inevitably contain several narrow defeats. Such a nemesis will emerge to haunt any bettor at some stage of her career if she concentrates on backing higher-priced selections to win.

Horse races are often decided in the most unpredictable of ways and by the narrowest of margins. How many times can you remember making the right selection for the wrong reasons? I have often felt that the singular confidence which some backers feel in relation to their selections is out of kilter with reality. Even the most prolific bettors are so frequently wrong that I feel it is important to take a probabilistic view of the likely outcome of a race. When I make a selection, I never feel **utterly** confident that the horse I have chosen will win. Rather, my balanced assessment has led me to contend that the horse I have selected is more likely to win the race than any of its fellow runners. On occasion, my margin of preference is so slight that I feel unable to make a selection at all. In the context of this view, a place bet might be the more sensible decision. However, your choice depends upon the level of risk that you are personally comfortable with. Indubitably, the highest levels of profit will result from win betting. A stealth benefit of place-betting on the exchanges is the ability to lay horses at shorter prices. Whereas I would be very unlikely to lay a horse at 8/1 and risk losing eight times my stake, I would far more eagerly lay the animal to finish out of the places at 2/1. Many horses are all or nothing types, they will either run up to their expected level of form or finish nowhere. If you suspect that the latter is likely then, rather than laying the horse at the win price, take the favourable option to bet that the runner will not make the frame.

Time to consider the each-way option

MULTIPLE SELECTIONS IN A SINGLE RACE

An alternative method of spreading risk is to back several runners in the same race. This tactic renders you less susceptible to the 'accident' factor. Whereas I would never back a single horse priced at evens, I would consider spreading my stake over two or three horses in order to double my money. When you back several runners in a race you are effectively laying the others. Hence, I prefer the simpler option of laying the short-priced favourite. I would not advocate the backing of several horses in a race as a blanket approach to betting. Analyse the race as you would normally, and if your efforts yield two prominent selections that you cannot split then there may be a case for dividing your stakes between them. Not every race will present a suitable opportunity and there will be fewer races still that yield three possible selections.

It should go without saying that I avoid backing highly fancied runners when making more than one selection in a race just as I would when backing a single horse. Hence, I would back two 4/1 runners but not a 15/8 shot coupled with a 6/1 horse. The stake should be spread over the different runners in such a way that a similar profit is returned regardless of which horse wins. The overall stake that you use in the race should be determined in the usual way and will reflect the fact that your strike rate will typically be higher than when backing individual horses. It is tempting to adjust your stakes so that the return yielded by backing one of your selections is greater than the return produced by the others. However, this should be avoided for the reasons I have already explained in the section on staking. If you are much less confident about one of your picks then why are you backing it at all? The whole principle underlying this type of betting manoeuvre is that it should be undertaken when you are equally confident that all the selections which you have made in a race represent good bets. Once again, your tendency to back different horses in the same race reflects your overall stance on risk and reward.

SELECTIVITY

A vital ingredient in the bettor's temperament is the patience required to refrain from betting until a suitable opportunity arises. Nobody is forcing you to bet and you must realise that not every race will present a viable opportunity. One practice that can help you to resist the temptations of betting unwisely is the laying down of personal rules or guidelines that describe the circumstances under which you are willing to bet. At the start of a period of betting, you may wish to formalise these pre-conditions in the manner that political parties set out manifestos prior to an election; the difference being that unlike them, you intend to keep your promises. For instance, you may observe that your record in bumpers is poor and thus elect to avoid such races. Rules operate as affirmations that reinforce your conviction to bet in a certain way. In betting, discrimination is a virtue. Indeed, if a good backer entered the dating game then he would never 'play the field,' instead he would assume an altogether more discerning approach. This analogy is not as far-fetched as it might seem, Freud contended that gambling is a displacement for sexual activity. Both practices do incorporate a process of selection and a thrilling climax (occasionally).

RACING MEDIA

In racing and betting, information truly is power. Being better informed not only makes a vast difference to your betting performance but it also increases your enjoyment and appreciation of the sport by making you feel connected to it. The information provided in the *Racing Post* affords an excellent overview. The various interviews and features can prove highly informative and allow you to 'touch base' with racing. However, from the serious backer's point of view, the racing press is like fast food whereas a detailed formbook represents balanced nutrition. If you can operate a computer then it is highly advisable to subscribe to a service that allows you to download an electronic formbook.

- Detailed form can be updated on a daily basis.
- The database can be instantaneously filtered and sorted in a variety of ways to suit the user.
- Declarations and entries for future races can be perused.
- A variety of pertinent statistics can be requested at the touch of a button.
- In order to test new systems and ideas, several years of past results can be queried

I subscribe to *Raceform Interactive* which is the market-leading electronic formbook and would recommend that you do the same. The pound a day or so that it costs is a thoroughly justified expense. The cynics might cry out that this is a Raceform book so of course I'm going to plug their product. In response, I merely have to point out that authors who write for Raceform's rival publishers also commend *Raceform Interactive* just as strongly without any incentive to do so. Case closed.

TIPPING SERVICES

"A poor man became rich because on me he bet"
The Jungle Brothers, rappers

If you have ever thought of relying on a tipping service then you must make this decision with both eyes open. There are some genuine tipsters who provide good advice but their opinion often burns a hole in the market and obtaining a good price can be as hard as selling shares during a stock market crisis. It is hard enough to make a profit when acting independently. The very nature of the market means that winning money is prohibitively difficult when betting in tandem with a large group of similarly-informed backers. In fact, I find that one of the real pitfalls in what I do is the risk that a popular tipster will coincide with my opinion and effectively blow my cover. When this happens, I am sometimes forced to reluctantly abandon a bet altogether. One of the worst feelings in betting is to carefully research a selection only to open up the *Racing Post* in the morning and find that Pricewise has come to the same conclusion. The decision not to bet is a clear one in that a loss of two points (e.g., 6/1 down to 4/1) on every bet that I strike would be enough to turn my modest profits into losses over the course of a year.

On some occasions it is possible to verify a tipster's past performance, but even when you do this it is amazing how often your decision to join a service coincides with a disastrous month. Very quickly, your hopes of making a profit turn into hopes of recouping your losses. Hence, you would need to assume a long-term view and be very confident of your decision to follow a given source of advice over several months. Contrary to popular opinion, individuals with successful betting histories or profitable systematic methods do sell their selections owing to the fact that such income is guaranteed and attended by little risk whereas betting income can never be. Personally, I would feel as if I was cutting my own throat and I would resent competing with others to obtain prices about horses that I had selected for them. In conclusion, I would advise you to follow tipping services as a last resort. If losing money due to a failure in your own judgement is psychologically difficult, then letting someone else lose it for you must be agonising.

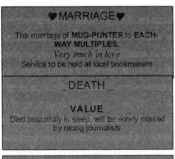

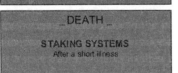

READING

Despite the importance of forming your own opinion, it is essential to familiarise yourself with the literature on betting and horse racing. Each author has a unique perspective and philosophy from which you will be able to glean vital knowledge.

Even the most dire and formulaic book will contain an idea or premise that is worthy of your attention. On occasion, I am enlightened not by what the author writes but what he fails to write; his train of thought infers an idea that I set out to test. Profitable backers thrive on ideas, and availing oneself of the betting literature will ignite those creative thought processes.

Alan Potts

There are only two authors whose books I would regard as essential reading and their names are Nick Mordin and Alan Potts. Concerning Nick Mordin, his perennial tome *Betting for a Living* is a definitive text. If you wish to develop a particular interest in speed ratings, paddock watching, or betting systems, then he has obliged by writing books on these subjects as well. In particular, *Winning Without Thinking* is the best book on the subject of betting that I have read to date. Alan Potts writes a good book, and the two he has authored to date are very insightful. If you have to choose between them, then plump for the larger and more recent *Inside Track*.

PRACTICAL CONSIDERATIONS

"Chance favours the prepared mind" **Louis Pasteur**

As a resource, time is fast becoming as scarce as money in modern society. We live in an age of internet shopping, microwave meals, fast-track promotions, crash courses, and speed dates that are inexorably followed by speed marriages. Yet is anything getting done faster? The average speed of cars in the centre of London is exactly what it was in 1900: 11 miles per hour. Set against this backdrop, a real concern for most bettors will be time management. Very few make a living solely from gambling, myself included. Thus, a balance will need to be achieved between your betting activities and occupation not to mention the rest of your life.

Rather than dovetail your sporting interests with your working life as some do, it is preferable to partition them. I set aside pockets of time during which I can focus on the task at hand and consider forthcoming races: afternoons, evenings; a whole week in the case of the Cheltenham festival. To produce profit in the long term normally requires that you make periodic investments of time in order to undertake research and planning, the fruits of which are only enjoyed over the following months. Any time spent in preparation is golden and sets the scene for either success or failure. Accordingly, it is best to work where you feel comfortable and will be undisturbed for considerable periods; not necessarily at home. What is certain is that one needs to deliberately set time aside and to be selfish about these periods. For example, think of how you go about ensuring that you honour appointments made with your doctor.

In terms of equipment, most new computers possess a level of performance more than adequate to betting requirements. The speed of the processor should not be a particular issue if buying a new machine. Otherwise, a CPU with a speed of 2 gigahertz or more is desirable. More important is the RAM, which serves as the computer's short-term or working memory space. A large amount of RAM is required, especially when handling large quantities of data in research and formbook applications. I recommend at least 1024 MB (just over 1 gigabyte) with any more serving as icing on the cake. In most cases, this amount of memory would require an upgrade even if buying a new machine. Apple computers are particularly efficient at numerical applications and it is possible to install as many as eight gigabytes of RAM into some of their better units. Most essential of all is a fast broadband internet connection to enable the downloading of racing data and for betting purposes.

A laptop is especially useful on the move although I have only once seen one being used by a punter at the races. The young lad was huddled under the main stand at Kempton in February, feverishly calculating probabilities of some kind while a procession of drunken louts teetered by spilling their Tetleys as they went. It has always struck me as more sensible to perform this type of operation by linking up with a third party using a mobile telephone. The nominated anchor person would be able to relay exchange prices and other information directly to my earpiece before placing bets on my behalf. Whereas mobile phones are not allowed in the betting ring, it is quite acceptable to use them in other areas of the course.

Time must also be set aside prior to a day's racing in order to identify betting opportunities and appraise the markets. I find the evening before a race presents the best opportunity to prepare myself. It may take longer than expected to arrive at a betting decision. Hence, if you leave the task until the morning of the race then not only will you become distracted by the prospect of the forthcoming journey (if attending the racecourse) but you may simply run out of time. I generally wait until the on-course betting market opens before placing a wager. This means that I can take advantage of a stronger market and be sure of the runners and the condition of the ground. Nevertheless, it is interesting to follow the exchange prices in the period after the 24-hour declarations are made and have the option to bet if I consider that a very favourable price can be obtained.

Exchange prices oscillate considerably in the day leading up to a big race and are affected by any corollary markets such as those of traditional bookmakers and spread betting firms. Market activity is also strongly affected by the *Racing Post* and the preview television programmes that are broadcast on the morning of the race. The best way to benefit from these fluctuations is to gain experience in the exchange market. If you set yourself up on the evening before a race then you are already attuned to certain prices and can follow them for an extended period.

The importance of attending race meetings cannot be underestimated. In particular, the opportunity to observe horses in the flesh greatly facilitates your understanding of the sport. Without regular on-course attendance you will always be betting with one arm tied behind your back. Pay heed to John McCririck's emphatic petition and COME RACING!

John McCririck

I have every angle covered. I deliberately allow myself a lot of time so that the trip to the course is as unstressful as possible. Fighting your way through traffic jams, running for trains, getting lost, or becoming stuck in a muddy car park are not conducive to the relaxed and alert frame of mind that one requires for betting. By allowing myself a lot of time I guard against unexpected occurrences such as traffic jams and train delays. This practice also ensures that I arrive in plenty of time to get my bearings. I plan my route beforehand if necessary so as to make sure that nothing needs to be catered for at the time. Good local knowledge of the racecourse and the surrounding area is also a bonus. For example, if approaching Cheltenham by road from the east (i.e., London) there is a turn-off from the A40 approximately three miles before the town that allows one to cut through the hills and approach the course from Cleeve Hill in the north, thus completely avoiding the gargantuan traffic jams. Cheltenham city centre is always to be avoided as it has quite possibly the most perplexing one-way system in the western world.

Here are a few more checkpoints
- Wear appropriate clothing
- Get a full night's sleep prior to racing
- Eat a filling yet digestible meal prior to arriving at the racecourse in order to

provide energy throughout the afternoon
- Take some snack food along to keep your energy levels high without having to join long queues and pay cheeky prices for dubious confectionary
- Ensure you have enough cash to bet with and not very much more
- Ensure that your mobile phone has enough charge

In short, it is good to develop a routine similar to the one a footballer might follow on a matchday in order to control that which is controllable. In this manner you'll instil confidence and be able to focus optimally on your betting. If this is all starting to sound a bit pedantic then bear in mind that once a pattern of behaviour has been established, it need require no real effort at all. With regards to clothing in the colder months, I use skin-tight gloves that I bought from a winter sports shop. They allow me to read my notes, handle money, and use my mobile phone easily when most people are suffering with the cold and missing bets. Good headgear is another must during the winter; if pushed I would rather look slightly eccentric than spend the afternoon in discomfort. Conversely, in the summer it is beneficial not to overdress. Once I have infiltrated the gates at Royal Ascot and escaped the withering stares of those officious bullies in bowler hats, my jacket and tie more often than not end up being 'left' somewhere near one of the bars. Additionally, I find good sunglasses and a hat that provides shade to be essential kit in the summer. Whatever clothes you wear, they should be comfortable and allow you to move around the course and betting ring with as much speed as you can muster.

Try to think ahead on raceday

It is very difficult at the larger meetings to achieve the great triumvirate of a close paddock inspection, a full appraisal of the betting ring, and a good view of the race. In practice, I tend to sacrifice the latter somewhat in order to concentrate on the paddock and in particular, the betting ring. There is a rather fine line between making a full parade ring inspection and missing the opportunity to place a bet. For obvious reasons, the betting ring is a priority. I take up a position around the parade ring that will afford me both a good view and the opportunity of a fast exit. The ringing of the bell that summons the jockeys to mount their rides is my cue to head for the betting ring. Once again, familiarity with the layout of the course can pay dividends on busier days. The type of access that you have is also significant. At Aintree's Grand National meeting, if you don't have admittance to one of the stands, which permits quick passage between the betting ring and the parade ring (which is half way to Ormskirk), then you might as well go and jump in the Mersey. In fairness to the Liverpudlian course, a rebuilding programme that is currently under way will improve matters.

The racecourse is a place where ideas often come to you and it is certainly a good tactic to commit these observations to memory for future reference. I record such musings on my mobile phone using a feature that most handsets now have. I had been using a digital voice recorder that I was rather proud of. Unfortunately, my use of the device tended to unnerve people around me who caught sight of me speaking covertly into my cupped hand and drew the conclusion that I was either schizophrenic, some sort of terrorist, or far worse, a policeman. Following one such misunderstanding, I did have to explain myself to a real officer of the law.

One of the most enjoyable elements of racing, as the sport's anthropologist Kate Fox has detailed, is the uniquely sociable climate of the racecourse. I really enjoy entering into a bit of banter and striking up conversations with those that I meet on course. Having writ this, it is a mistake to take casual or virgin racegoers with you on a betting mission as they will prove too much of a distraction. The pattern of events typically resembles the following: Initially, you are lionised as a betting guru and persecuted with endless queries. The general expectation is that you will single-handedly bring about the collapse of the bookmaking industry on that very afternoon. Subsequently, each of your selections fails to even complete the course and your strongest bet of the day has to be put down in front of the stands. Meanwhile, your colleagues are nonchalantly finding every winner under the sun using various folk-techniques ranging from the "pick the one with the best name" system to the "bet on Frankie" method. By the end of the afternoon your friends have started to regard you with a mixture of deep sympathy and mistrust and nobody can bring themselves to look you in the eye for a couple of weeks afterwards. On the contrary, to go betting with the like-minded is actually a boon as you can confer and sound out ideas.

COUNTER INTUITION

Because racing revolves around the enigmatic phenomenon of equine performance, opinion is very pervasive and racing is infested with experts. However, what sort of knowledge really holds currency? The blizzard of information that exists in the racing media today can often serve to obscure genuine insight. A premise is not true merely because it is contained in a published book such as this one. Nor is an opinion excused from being nonsense simply because it is credited to a well-known racing 'personality'.

An essential building block of your betting success will be your ability to form your own opinions and judiciously accept or reject those of others under advisement. The principle that I am referring to is expressed well in the following tale: In a rural village, a farmer goes out in search of an escaped donkey. He calls at various properties in vain before finally visiting the residence owned by the officious local constable. The policeman is in the yard at the front of his house as the farmer approaches him with trepidation to enquire, "we've lost a donkey up at the farm, have you seen it?" "Why no" replied the policeman. At that moment, a donkey could be heard braying from behind the policeman's house. "Then what's that?" retorted the farmer. "Now who would you rather believe", bellowed the constable, "an officer of the law or a donkey!" If you want to make money from betting then you have got to believe the donkey! In other words, you are risking your own capital so base your decisions on what your senses tell you not those of others.

The odds that you will be able to obtain about a selection depend on the betting public's opinion. Hence, backing fancied horses will drastically reduce your ability to show a profit. Conversely, if you can lay horses that are given too much respect by the punting masses then you might profit from their ignorance. The spirit of this approach was captured by Alan Potts, who wrote a book entitled *Against the Crowd* in which he demonstrated the necessity of opposing the popular viewpoint in order to achieve a profit.

Like most others, I started out thinking that the goal of betting on horses was answering the question "which horse is going to win this race". It is clear to me now that picking winners is merely a starting point. I gradually adopted the view that the only way to show consistent profits was to back horses that were undervalued by the betting public. As time goes by, I am beginning to take this approach to its logical conclusion and turn the whole problem on its head. Rather than focussing on form analysis or methods of selection, I am studying the betting public itself. If I can expose a flaw or prejudice in conventional wisdom then I will have identified a chink in the market's armour that I can exploit. This ethos succeeds because the herd instinct is so strong: Categorical, unquestioning, collective thinking is one of the hallmarks of our society.

The sort of counter-intuitive thought processes that are required in betting are equally applicable to other walks of life. Once in a while I catch the train from Waterloo to Richmond at around five o'clock on a weekday afternoon. As Waterloo is the principal terminus serving a massive tranche of South West London, the train I usually catch is bristling with commuters. I often arrive at Waterloo with only two or three minutes to spare, so getting a seat on the train can be quite difficult. I recall one occasion when I walked onto the platform, saw that the first two carriages of the train were nearly full and resolved to stride to the very end of the train where I expected to find more space to sit down. The problem was that everyone else had done exactly the same and the front coach was like a train in Calcutta; people all but hanging from the sides and sitting on the roof. The whistle blew and I had to squeeze into a space that was designed for a much smaller man or preferably a child. I had cause to remember with a wry smile that I had walked swiftly past plenty of unoccupied seats on the second carriage that I could have simply sat down on. Next time I faced similar conditions I remembered what had happened and took up a seat on the first carriage I saw. From this berth I was able to watch hordes of people galloping earnestly up the platform all being impeded by a fat man with large cases who kept stopping; in a horse race there would have been a stewards enquiry. The point of this frankly silly anecdote is that, in finding a seat on the train, I had found an 'edge' that exploited a common misapprehension, namely that there must always be more seats at the end of the train because it is further to walk there.

In practice, I have found that the strongest determinant of the betting public's collective opinion is the menagerie of tips that are found in the *Racing Post* newspaper. A huge number of backers on course, in betting shops, and at home read the 'Spotlight' race preview that appears underneath the jockey's colours. I have often observed that the single horse, which spotlight is obliged to nominate for each race, receives indiscriminate support. When your own assessment of the race leads you to believe that spotlight's selection is unlikely to win, you have located a good opportunity to lay a short-priced horse. If you require similar fodder then look at the horses that have been napped by the weaker tipsters at the foot of the naps table in the *Racing Post*.

GAMEPLANS – A BIT FISHY?

The title of this section is dedicated to someone who reviewed the first edition of *Against the Odds*, apparently without having read it, and bemoaned the lack of a 'gameplan' – another of those American phrases I love so much. I certainly took the point that the second edition required a clear, concise summary so I have endeavoured to include one here. By asking for a 'gameplan' the reviewer inadvertently raised a really valid point. My somewhat deflating riposte is that betting is a domain where there can be no simple formula for winning money.

As authors before me have realised, writing about profitable betting approaches is self-defeating if not futile. As soon as you report a way of making money, bettors will begin to incorporate your prescription into their armoury and it will cease to be profitable. Hence, the very notion of a fixed gameplan does not really tessellate with the fluid nature of betting at all. To return to the rather odd subject of quantum physics, the betting angles that I have reported in this book are quite like certain sub-atomic particles that, once created, can only exist for microseconds before rapidly decaying. Bearing all of the above in mind, why bother declaring that backing all juvenile top-rated sprinters yielded a profit of 17p per pound staked? The answer is that by showing you what has been profitable in the past I have been demonstrating how to research what will produce positive returns in the future. More important still is the mindset that underlies this endeavour. Better to show someone how to fish, than simply to give him a solitary fish as they say.

A worry that afflicts many gamblers who have understood the way of things is "where is the next profitable approach going to come from"? This need not be a concern because, as the elastic betting market shifts to close one loophole, it surely creates a new opening ready to be exploited. The best analogy I can think of is that of the musical composer who wonders if all the best pieces have already been written. Of course, this fear is illusory. In fifty years time there will be a wealth of new music and a future musician will then once more wonder if all the best music has already been created. Remembering the words of my late grandfather, I don't worry about where the next profitable system will come from: "There's as good fish in the sea as what came out of it," he used to say. I have noticed that this applies quite well to romantic partners too.

Anyway, for those who like potted summaries and bullet points, here are a few fishing tips:

- Set time aside for planning and research. Make clear decisions about the approach you are going to follow, under exactly what conditions you will bet, how long you will follow the approach for, what stakes you will use, and how big your betting bank will be.
- Keep records and analyse your own strengths and weakness so as to learn from your triumphs and disasters.
- Do everything in your power to familiarise yourself with computers. At the very least, use a computer to keep your records and access an electronic formbook.
- Never bet at odds on. Establish a range of odds that you will accept: for example, 4/1 to 8/1. Bet longshots with caution and only as a small part of your overall strategy.

- If you lose your natural passion for betting and racing then stop and do something else that you enjoy.
- Be selective in terms of which types of races you follow and exercise your prerogative of refraining from betting in some races. To bet on two races in a card is plenty, sometimes one race, sometimes three. You might learn something from the races you don't bet on that will help you win next time.
- Specialise to maximise profits. If time is limited, then follow a single approach assiduously rather than trying to keep several different plates spinning.
- Give yourself adequate time to research the runners before betting at a meeting and plan your day carefully.
- Keep in mind the random nature of results and accept the inevitable reality of frequent losses. Also, reconcile yourself to the fact that you will sometimes lose money in a manner that will seem 'unlucky'. Try to keep a balanced perspective by also remembering the times when you benefited from good fortune.
- Be careful not to let the results of previous bets disturb you emotionally and affect how you bet. Bet the same whether you have just had a big win or an unfortunate defeat.
- There are plenty of opportunities to make money from all-weather and National Hunt racing; try to keep an open mind. It may also pay to show an interest in foreign form that has a direct bearing on British racing; French, Irish, and increasingly German form for example.
- Come racing!
- Don't forget to lay horses as well as backing them. Consider the place and each-way options. Also it may pay to back multiple runners in the same race.
- Keep it simple. Exotic bets that rely on multiple selections are best given a wide berth. Dabble with these if you want to add some interest to a sport you are watching and don't mind losing some money.
- Read racing books.
- Subscribe to an electronic form service.
- Picking winners is just the start. Focus your attention on the machinations of the betting market and aim to identify commonly-held betting prejudices that can be exploited for profit.

During the course of this book, I have unearthed many profitable betting approaches. Here is a reminder of some of the trends that you might want to consider when having a bet.

Why not try laying short-priced favourites who meet the following criteria:

- Running in races with 20 or more runners
- Rated 10 lb or more behind the top-rated runner in the race
- Carrying a high weight in long-distance races (3m 2f +)
- Fillies and mares carrying heavy weights under National Hunt rules
- Running during first few weeks of flat season
- Trainer on a 0% strike rate from last 10 runners
- Top-rated yet ridden by a jockey with a 0% recent strike rate
- Heavily-weighted runners running on soft or heavy ground
- Two-year-olds making their racecourse debuts
- Underexposed handicappers (few races during last 3 months)
- Drawn on the outside in races around sharp turns

Also, why not consider backing runners that fit these descriptions:

- Top-rated two-year-olds
- Runners that have been narrowly beaten in non-handicaps on their latest start
- Martin Pipe's runners when his recent strike rate is high
- National Hunt horses below the age of nine following a move to a new stable
- Horses running on soft ground that have shown a marked preference for similar conditions
- Top-rated runners on the flat when the going is firmer than good
- Rides taken over by Leighton Aspell
- Any ride taken over by a different jockey in National Hunt races (Class D +)
- Horses running at Uttoxeter following a run at Chepstow
- Top-rated runners in non-handicaps that finished out of the first nine places on their most recent start. Use speed ratings on previous start to determine the top-rated horse
- Pay extra attention to top-rated runners with a Raceform rating of 110 or more.

CHAPTER 23
Betting Ethos

The specifics of selection and betting are like bricks in a wall, but what holds them together? You do. Betting is a skill and as such, it can be learned. However, the ability to be a consistently profitable backer depends very much on the content of your character. A truism that one often encounters among serious betting folk is that there are probably more rocket scientists than professional gamblers. You must have a spark of ambition to ignite your attempt. However, the slow burning compound that will fuel your ascent is self-belief. The inner confidence of the backer is much like that of the successful athlete, a determination to prevail and give whatever is required of them; the surety that, whatever happens, failure will not spring from lack of effort.

If there were a pantheon of great sporting coaches it would contain Vince Lombardi, the talismanic trainer of the Green Bay Packers, a championship-winning American football team. He said that confidence when you're winning is not really confidence because everyone is confident when they're winning. Rather, confidence is to keep one's faith when defeat is looming. A losing run is the ultimate test of your confidence. It is incumbent upon you to withstand the force of the blows and keep placing those bets, measure for measure because you believe what you are doing is right. In the longer course of your betting career, defeats are inevitable but it should not follow that you are *defeated*; there is a great difference between losing and **being** a loser.

The adversity that you face makes you who you are. Think of coal and diamonds, both consist of pure carbon, but the carbon in diamonds has suffered a lot more; it has been subjected to many more years of much greater pressure from the weight of the rock above it. Yet diamonds are infinitely hard and beautiful whereas coal is dirty and relatively worthless. It is amazing how many famously successful individuals have sprung from adversity. If you've read a few biographies in your time then you'll know what I mean. If you're going to be a successful backer (forgive me for assuming that you're not one already!) then you need to be able to make a commitment and go the distance, just like a Grand National winner. I have forgotten who said it takes twenty years of hard work to become an overnight sensation, but it was a good point that they made.

"Excellence is not an act but a habit" **Aristotle**

There is something almost Zen-like about the equanimity of a successful backer. One who meets with triumph and disaster and treats those two impostors just the same as Rudyard Kipling wrote. Indeed, Kipling must have been a betting man because he went on to write:

If you can make one heap of all your winnings
And risk it on one turn of pitch-and-toss,
And lose, and start again at your beginnings
And never breath a word about your loss.

Would it not be wonderful if all gamblers refrained from 'breathing a word about their loss'! In any case, a certain stoicism and indifference serve the backer well. The sports writer Raymond Smith observed that the 'high-rollers' of the turf must have iced water in their veins instead of blood. Some gamblers I know must have iced water on their brains!

It helps to gain perspective by contemplating the true value of money. It is only when you have experienced and lost that which is beyond monetary value that you can be dispassionate about the prospect of losing money. Ironically, in order to secure the goal of winning money you need to almost disregard its value. I achieve this by having what I call 'gaff bets', which are so called because they are fairly whimsical in nature and consist of a mere £2 stake. According to Kate Fox's research, using such a small stake brings my masculinity in to question! This is the same amount that I staked when I used to skive off school with my friends and sneak into Yarmouth races, to whom I now issue a frank and unconditional apology. I make these light-hearted bets in the same way I have always done: After a quick scan of the *Racing Post*, a sniff round the paddock, and a frenzied charge around the ring in the style of a pinball. Once the bet is struck, I poodle off down to the running rails and shout louder than is socially acceptable whilst beating a rolled-up copy of the *Racing Post* into my cupped fist like a paper whip.

I celebrate winners in a giddy-delirium of pogo-ing and whooping and can be heard to cheer the winning jockey back to the paddock with riotous shouts of "Yes my son!", although it is generally understood that I am not the rider's natural parent. If there is a mug punter in all of us then I am merely allowing mine to express himself in a healthy and appropriate manner so that he doesn't intrude upon my proper betting. I can indulge all my prejudices just like everyone else. Sometimes I back Mick Fitzgerald's mounts in jump races because I believe him to be my 'lucky jockey', plus I like the sound of yelling "C'mon Mick Fitz!". Gaff bets are my bizarre answer to the awkwardness that some serious backers feel about travelling to the racecourse in order to bet in a single race. They also ensure that I maintain my enthusiasm for racing by partaking of the rituals that are constitutive of it. In so doing, I have never lost sight of the reason I fell in love with horseracing. I find it quite easy to draw a clear distinction between my serious betting and my jovial jaunts into mugpunterdom. Thus, I have found my own unique way of being emotionally detached, because I sublimate all my baser instincts into my gaff betting.

When I first started using relatively large stakes (over £100), I found the process of witnessing the races quite stressful, and stress is an emotion that you need to aggressively eliminate from your betting life. If you place large bets (by your own standards) on a very frequent basis then you need to do so without trepidation. The solution that I found to this problem was to simply not watch the races. As I was placing most of my bets off-course, this practice did not present a problem for me. It depends entirely on your approach: If you're a systematic backer, then the intricacies of the race will not interest you. However, if you follow a more enlightened path, then it is important to ascertain to what extent your predictions were proven accurate. This process is not unlike the training a neural network undergoes and it is essentially the way we develop knowledge of racehorse performance.

There is a stereotype of the professional backer watching almost with disinterest as his £1000 bet falls at the last fence while ten lengths clear of the field. This example is a bit far fetched and few achieve the aim of repressing their feelings to such an extent. On the first day of the 2002 Cheltenham festival, I was standing on the rails when *Valiramix* went down. It so happened that the quiet man standing next to me had placed the most enormous bet on the tragic horse, even by the standards of professional backers betting at the Cheltenham festival. He turned to me, smiled a wistful smile and said, "It'll come back to me, it always does" and from the look in his eyes, I had no reason to disbelieve him.

It is healthy to feel some degree of emotion, but the important consideration is that you manage those feelings effectively. Hence, on the rare occasions that I lose a bet due to apparent misfortune I am disappointed, but not to the extent that my afternoon is spoiled or my thinking becomes clouded. Conversely, if I win then I do celebrate. After all, that is what all the hard work is for. I am confident that the winners will continue to come over time. Hence, when they do arrive, I might as well mark those occasions. There is an indescribable feeling when your predictions are proved correct. Psychologists would refer to a 'flow experience' of optimal absorption, footballers would relate the sensation to the scoring of an important goal and they might say that it is 'better than sex', a Zen monk would speak of the 'satori experience' that attends a moment of great enlightenment, religious men would cite divine intervention … for me it's a winning bet. My own sedate form of celebration has become rather ritualised and involves a Cuban cigar. Do you remember the inescapable dénouement that concluded each episode of the *A-team* when Hannibal would be heard to croon "I love it when a plan comes together"; well that is the mood of the moment, just without the sinister leather gloves.

Time has shown that successful backers are those who carve niches for themselves. History is replete with opportunities in betting that flared up momentarily and then expired. Draw biases, the old each-way fractions, and the straight forecast formula provided incisive backers with a doorway to profits that was firmly shut by the time that word had spread to all and sundry. That is why the backer is always adapting to circumstances in order to find his edge. The essential nature of the market ensures that only those who follow the path less trodden will prevail. If every backer were as astute as a professional, then a lone mug punter would probably have the edge! That is why you need to exercise lateral thinking.

The successful backers that I have had the fortune to meet were all very much individuals who lived by their own rules. The uncertainties attached to betting may be iniquitous, but nobody forces you to choose them. You must possess a degree of self-reliance and integrity because if you fail there can only be one person responsible – yourself. The singularity of purpose that is required to achieve such ends can be very consuming. I took a lot of comfort from reading that Tony McCoy's idea of a good night out was preparing for the next day's racing! I admire the way he manages to be himself in a world where pressures abound to be otherwise. Making a consistent profit from betting has none of the rewards of being a top-jockey, not even the financial ones. Nevertheless, backers can still learn something from the willpower and self-belief of the steely, unpretentious Irishman. In the end, it doesn't matter what you choose to do but the way in which you achieve your goals. Muhammad Ali was quoted as saying that if he had been a dustman instead of a boxer, he would have been the best dustman in the world, and who would disagree with that.

In the final analysis, successful people are those who are brave enough to gamble in life. Such individuals would rather have a whole duck for dinner or go hungry as it were; find true love or be alone. There are those who take risks and lose, but at least they gave themselves a chance to fulfil their potential, whereas those who sat smugly on the fence did not even have a ticket for the raffle. We are all gamblers; even by living we risk death. Life is much like a casino, and we all know that the house always wins in the end. However, it is only those who have failed to take advantage of the opportunities that life has given them who really fear death. Some psychologists would say that your self-esteem and, to a lesser extent your happiness, are in direct proportion to your willingness to take risks. If you have dared to reach out and touch your dreams then you can have no regrets and this is a most enviable state.

The graph which appeared at the start of the previous chapter demonstrated that even if you are ultimately successful, the road to profits is a winding one. Patience is an important attribute to possess because the wins will inevitably be outnumbered by losses. When you adopt a betting approach you are taking a long-term view. Your ultimate success will be like the climatic changes that accompany the seasons and general runs of form will be like warm or cold fronts that move in from time to time. The outcomes of individual bets are akin to sudden showers or sunny spells; even summer contains many wet and dreary days. Your whole betting year is a bet in itself. When I set out to bet at the start of a season there is a remote chance that I will lose all my money. However, based on the information in Michael Adams' betting bank tables, I learn that the chance of doubling my money over the course of the flat season is something like 79.64% – that's a 1/4 shot! Now if you're a gambling man you'd recognise that those are very good odds indeed. If you're a gambling *woman* ... then I'd love to hear from you!

Glossary and Notes

Alan Potts: A professional backer and author.

Alex Bird: Read about Alex Bird and his contemporaries in Raymond Smith's *The High Rollers of the Turf* (1999, Blackwater Press).

Backer: One who backs (places a bet on) a horse.

Betting exchanges: Betting exchanges usurp the traditional role of the bookmaker by serving as intermediaries that allow bettors with opposing viewpoints to effectively bet against each other. Although betting exchanges typically operate through the medium of the internet, it is possible to place such bets by telephone also.

Breeders Cup: The Breeders Cup is a prestigious American race meeting that is held in late autumn. The fixture comprises championship flat races on dirt (the typical racing surface used in America) and on turf. More than any other meeting, the Breeders Cup attracts challengers from around the globe including a notable European contingent.

Cesarewitch: A long-distance handicap traditionally held on Newmarket's Rowley Mile course in the late autumn of each year. Runners drawn high or low have an appalling record whereas those drawn in the middle stalls are far more likely to win. The reason for this bias might be the width of the track at Newmarket and the corresponding necessity of being 'covered-up'.

Claiming a weight advantage: The mount of an apprentice or conditional jockey who is claiming a weight advantage carries three, five, or seven lbs less in weight than it would otherwise have done.

Classic: The five classics are the principal flat races of each season contested by three-year-old runners only. The 1000 guineas (fillies) and 2000 guineas (colts) are run over a mile at Newmarket (Rowley) in early May. The Oaks (fillies) and Derby (colts) are contested over 1m 4f at Epsom in early June, and the St. Leger is run over 1m 6f 132y at Doncaster in mid September.

Collateral form: If two horses have never raced against each other but have both raced against a third animal then one can use this 'collateral' form to infer how the two runners in question would fare against each other.

Colt: A colt is a male horse under the age of five that has not yet been castrated. Conversely, a filly is a female horse under the age of five, at which point she is designated a 'mare'.

Conditional riders: Conditionals are the National Hunt equivalent of the apprentice jockeys who ride on the flat.

Connections: The connections of a horse are those who have a shared interest in the animal, principally the owner(s), but to a less extent any person who is 'connected' with the horse in some way, e.g., the trainer, the head lad from the stable, etc. There is a discussion of the term 'connections' on page 76 of *The Racing Tribe* (1999, Metro).

David Ashforth: A racing journalist and backer who writes a highly respected and forthright Saturday column for the *Racing Post* and has authored an excellent gambling autobiography *Hitting the Turf* (1995, Headline).

Draw: A horse's allotted position in the starting stalls that are used in flat races.

Dr. Peter May: A writer on the subject of selection methods who has authored eight books including *Forecasting Methods for Horse Racing* (1998, Raceform).

Ebor handicap and the draw bias: Refer to page 56 of *Against the Crowd* (1995, Aesculus Press).

Form: When displayed in a newspaper, form (the record of previous performances) is often abbreviated into a series of numbers or characters, each representing a race. The races are listed in chronological order with the most recent race appearing on the far right of the list. The numbers represent the finishing position of the horse (e.g., 1 = finished 1st, 0 = finished 10th or worse). Alphabetic characters generally indicate a failure to complete the race (e.g., F = horse fell, P = horse was pulled-up). The form figures that I have listed in relation to myself indicate that I was an awful sprinter!

Gaff tracks: The smaller, more provincial racecourses are commonly referred to as the 'gaff' tracks.

Gelding: A horse that has been gelded (castrated).

Get on: To 'get on' is to successfully place a bet, i.e., to have it accepted.

The Guineas: See 'Classic'.

Kate Fox: In 1996, the BHB (British Horseracing Board) commissioned Kate Fox to undertake research on racegoers. The findings of this research are published in the superbly written and highly insightful book *The Racing Tribe* (1999, Metro).

Lay: To 'lay' a horse is to accept another's bet and therefore act in the role that is traditionally associated with the bookmaker. Hence, if you accept a bet of £10 on a horse whose odds stand at 10/1 then you will win the £10 stake should the horse lose but you will be liable to pay the £100 winnings to the other bettor if the horse does indeed win. To lay a horse is the opposite of backing it, which is to bet that the horse will win.

Lay-off: In order to reduce his liabilities, a bookmaker may elect to 'lay-off' part of a bet he has accepted by backing the same horse to win with another bookmaker. If the bookmaker manages to achieve the ideal of backing the horse in question at higher odds than those he offered himself then he is said to have 'got on velvet' because profit is ensured.

Layers: Bookmakers are sometimes referred to as layers.

Michael Adams: The author of *Secrets of Successful Betting* (2002, Raceform).

Miss Dorothy Paget: The eccentric aristocrat Miss Dorothy Paget was one of the most renowned backers in history, fearlessly placing 'telephone number' bets of as much as £10k in the 1930s.

Mudlark: A horse that is thought to prefer very soft ground.

Nap: A nap is one's principal selection. The word originates from the parlance of card games and is an abbreviation of Napoleon.

Naps table: The profit derived from backing the naps put forward by various newspaper tipsters is displayed in a table that can be found in the *Racing Post*.

Nietzsche: The reference to Friedrich Nietzsche comes from *The Gay Science*, written between 1878 and 1882.

Novices: Once a horse has recorded its first victory, it will relinquish its novice status from the beginning of the following season onwards. In 2004, the BHB remodelled the structure of novice chases by introducing three categories: beginner's chases for horses who have not won over fences, novice chases for horses rated 0-105, and 0-110 open novice chases.

Nursery: A handicap for two-year-old horses.

Peter Braddock: A jockey, trainer, owner, and writer on matters pertaining to racing. I refer to his book *'Braddock's Complete Guide to Horse Race Selection and Betting'* (1983, Longman).

Phil Bull: The enigmatic Phil Bull was a professional gambler of note who made his fortune largely by devising a method of producing ratings based on racetimes. Based on this principle, he sired the Timeform organisation, whose current managing director is Channel Four Racing's Jim McGrath.

Projected starting prices: The estimated starting prices which are printed in the racing press.

Rag: Rank outsider with no realistic chance of winning.

Risk: There is an excellent passage on the subject of risk in *The Racing Tribe* by Kate Fox, pages 147-8.

Risk taking by men and women: This finding was part of another research report by Kate Fox, this one relating to gender issues and risk-taking in the financial sphere. The report, entitled *Sex and the City*, was commissioned by Virgin Direct and was published in 2001.

Sex and betting: Refer also to *Against the Crowd*, page 113.

Single win bet: To back a single horse to win as opposed to combining multiple selections in the same bet.

Steeplechases: Steeplechases are commonly referred to as chases and horses that compete in these races are known as 'chasers'. The steeplechase draws its lineage from cross-country events that were staged between the church steeples of neighbouring towns.

Stuffing: To read more about the 'stuffing' of horses, refer to Sydney Harris' book *Horse Racing: The Essential Guide to Backing Winners* (2000, As-is publishing), page 4.

Sydney Harris: See 'Stuffing'.

Tattersalls: The mid-priced Tattersalls enclosure is typically situated between the members' enclosure (the most expensive) and the silver ring (least expensive). The name is taken from Richard Tattersall, who founded the world's first bloodstock auction house in 1766.

Tissue: The compilation of odds drawn up by industry representatives, upon which the on-course bookmakers base their initial prices.

Tote: 'Tote' is an abbreviation of 'the horserace totalisator board'; a pool-based betting system that was introduced to British racecourses in 1929. Part of the profit that the Tote produces is used to support racing.

Tote deductions for 'win' bets: If you spread a stake of £115.61 between all the runners in a given race and yours were the only bets then the 'win' pool would equal £100 after a 13.5% deduction.

Trouble the judge: The judge is a racecourse official who determines the finishing order of the runners and the distances that separate them. If a horse is involved in the competition for the higher places then the animal is said to have 'troubled the judge'.

Unexposed: The ability of horses with little public form (i.e., in races) cannot easily be assessed in comparison with their rivals. Such runners are said to be 'unexposed'.

Weak market: When there is very little betting activity, a market is said to be 'weak'. In such markets, prices are relatively static as there is little betting interest in the race.

Yard: A racing stable is commonly referred to as a 'yard'.

Appendix

As I reread the first edition of this book a few months after it was published in May 2003 there were several points at which the blood drained from my face and I thought to myself 'I wish I hadn't written that'. For some strange reason I chose to include this poem. Nevertheless, some people actually seemed to like it so it makes a reappearance albeit tucked away at the back of the book. Those of you who have been to the Festival will recognise the description. For those who haven't, I extend my deepest sympathies…

March brings mist on the hills above Cheltenham
The drumming of hooves on wind-beaten turf
Proclaims the advent of the mythic festival
Under timeless battleship-grey skies

A peaceful invasion of Range Rovers and Jaguars
Storms the brink of Cleeve Hill like armoured divisions.
We fortunate few, like pilgrims have travelled
And no man's journey is too long

Jubilant we flow into the crowd
A tributary into this teeming river of humanity
Catching our own wild delight in the eyes of strangers
For we have cheated time to be here once more

Memorial benches on the members' lawn
Each weather-beaten seat has a story to tell
"He enjoyed and contributed to Cheltenham racecourse"
He enjoys no longer yet he contributes still

Clans would clash upon these hillsides
And the blood of noble men was spilt in this vale
Where these new knights bear silks upon their armour
And ride into battle as once did warriors

Istabraq passes before us; an equine Messiah
His mane dancing like the headdress of an apache warrior
Charlie Swan rides proud and erect as a king of old legend
For today, the green and the gold are everyone's colours

The last hurdle stands gateway to their consummation
Beckoning with the promise of stolen glory
Like salmon leaping upstream they take flight
For an eternal instant to hang immortal

Deafening, the tumult of expectation
That transfuses their wracked bodies with bravery
And they storm the hill as if it were their true purpose
To reach up and touch the face of triumph

Almost as it is sounded, the roar dies in their throats
And they flee for the car park as if their liberty were at threat
As desperate to leave as they were to arrive
A serpentine procession of crimson brake lights and purring engines

Wrapped in the bosom of Cleeve, Prestbury falls silent
Betting slips carpet the ground like so many autumn leaves
Withered and strown across the shire
The snowfall of broken dreams upon which the dusk softly treads

As the gloaming reclaims the racecourse
I stand vigil atop the brow of Cleeve Hill, an islander
Helicopters ascend through the burnished golden twilight like fireflies
And all Gloucestershire lies glorious below me, bathed in the half-light